FEMINISM

REINVENTING the f-WORD

naDia aBusHanaB Higgins

TWENTY-FIRST CENTURY BOOKS / MINNEAPOLIS

In memory of my grandmothers, Pauline Scribner and Wadia Abushanab—both feminists before their time —N.A.H.

Twenty-First Century Books
A division of Lerner Publishing Group, Inc.
241 First Avenue North
Minneapolis, MN 55401 USA

For reading levels and more information, look up this title at www.lernerbooks.com.

Main body text set in Univers LT Std 57 Condensed 10/15.
Typeface provided by Adobe Systems.

Library of Congress Cataloging-in-Publication Data

Higgins, Nadia Abushanab.
    Feminism : reinventing the f-word / by Nadia Abushanab Higgins.
        pages cm
      Audience: Grade 6 to 12.
      Includes bibliographical references and index.
      ISBN 978-1-4677-6147-5 (lb : alk. paper) — ISBN 978-1-4677-9578-4 (eb pdf)
      1. Feminism—Juvenile literature. I. Title.
    HQ1190.H54 2016
    305.42—dc23   2015000898

Manufactured in the United States of America
1 – CG – 12/31/15

TaBLe Of cOntents

ARE YOU A
FEMINIST?

imagine it's March 5, 1961, an average day in the United States. Mrs. John Doe is at the hospital giving birth to a baby girl, who will automatically take her father's last name. The nurses at the hospital address the mother—whose first name is Jane—as Mrs. Doe (not Jane or Ms. Doe). Like most new mothers of the 1960s, Jane is in her twenties. Jane is white and middle class, so like other white, middle-class women, she finished college, got married, and became a full-time housewife. She does not have a job outside the home, spending an average of fifty-five hours a week doing household chores such as grocery shopping, meal preparation, mending clothes, and cleaning her house from top to bottom every day. With the birth of her first child, she will devote her time to caring for her home, her husband's needs, and her baby.

Women who have jobs outside the home in 1960s America, on the other hand, include a majority of women of color and white women of the working class. They make about fifty-nine cents for every dollar earned by men. Women clerk in stores, clean houses for other families, answer phones in offices, or serve meals in school lunchrooms. Women also fill the ranks of teachers and nurses. Yet even these highly skilled professions pay far less than traditional men's work, such as collecting garbage or driving a bus. Working women are also responsible for cooking and cleaning at their

The ideal American woman of the 1960s was a married, stay-at-home mother, often referred to as the Happy Homemaker. While many women did not fit this stereotype, or even want to, magazines and television shows and movies promoted the image as the only way to be a respectable woman.

own homes and taking care of their children. Women can't get loans or buy houses without a man to sign the paperwork with them.

On TV, boys and men are the protagonists, and girls and women are sisters, wives, and mothers. Or they play evil stepmothers, "bad" girls who've lost their way, or femmes fatales who bring doom upon the men they encounter. At school, girls learn to sew and cook in home economics class, while boys work with metal and wood in shop class. There are no organized or professional sports for girls, except if you count cheerleading. One of a teen girl's main jobs is to avoid sex and protect her virginity. She doesn't want to get a bad reputation and ruin her chances at marriage. As for lesbians, gay men, and transgender Americans, they're definitely in the closet.

For women and teen girls who do have sex, the birth control pill has just been invented, but the side effects range from nausea and weight gain to depression and strokes. Many doctors refuse to prescribe it to unmarried women. If a teen girl does get pregnant, she may choose an abortion, which is illegal—and dangerous. If she gets raped or if she is the victim of domestic violence, she has almost no legal recourse to bring her attacker to justice. In North Carolina, for example, she's permitted to file rape charges only if she's a virgin—though how her lawyers prove that is not entirely clear.

A book by Betty Friedan, *The Feminine Mystique* (1963), put words to the boredom, resentment, and unhappiness that many women and girls feel about the social and legal limits on their lives. Partly as a result of this best-selling book, a new wave of feminism, building on the women's rights movement of the previous decades, takes off.

FROM THEN TO NOW

Fast-forward to the twenty-first century. For women and girls, men too, the decade of the 1960s seems like life on another planet. Women now make up half of the US workforce. They account for one-third of all doctors and lawyers and fill just over half of all managerial and professional jobs. Forty percent of US mothers are the family breadwinners. Women have begun to outpace men in advanced degrees so quickly that some universities are worried about recruiting enough men.

Twenty-first-century girls see plenty of fictional females—from Katniss Everdeen to Veronica Mars—taking charge on-screen. Girls are reclaiming domestic arts such as sewing and knitting, not in preparation for being

Betty Friedan (1921–2006) was an icon of the second wave of the feminist movement in the United States. A graduate of Smith College in Massachusetts, she worked as a journalist before starting a family in the 1940s. Unhappy in her role as a housewife, she surveyed other graduates of Smith to see if they shared her dissatisfaction. Her discoveries led to her book *The Feminine Mystique* (1963), which challenged the myth of the Happy Homemaker and is considered one of the most influential nonfiction works of the twentieth century.

Maya Moore of the Minnesota Lynx goes up for a layup during a Western Conference semifinals game against the San Antonio Stars in 2014. Women's participation in amateur and professional sports has skyrocketed as a result of federal legislation that came out of the feminist movement in the early 1970s to prohibit gender-based discrimination in sports, education, and other federally funded programs.

wives and mothers but as fun, funky hobbies. They're trying out for soccer, basketball, football, hockey, and volleyball teams in droves. They're joining professional sports teams such as the Phoenix Mercury, the 2014 champions of the Women's National Basketball Association (WNBA), and they're hitting a hole in one at pro golf tournaments.

Women have far more sexual freedom, and being an out lesbian is no big deal for millions of women. In fact, same-sex marriage is legal across the nation, so thousands of lesbian couples head to courthouses and to churches and temples to get married. Meanwhile, gender categories are breaking wide open, as transgender people gain visibility and legal rights. For millions of women, birth control is cheap, easy to buy and use, and safe. Abortion for those who choose the procedure is also legal and safe. Domestic violence is no longer a private matter but has become a punishable crime. A rape survivor can dial a crisis hotline and take her abuser to court.

And yet . . .

Halted Progress

In the United States, a rape is reported every 6.2 minutes, and 98 percent of rapists avoid prison sentences. On campus, one out of five women experience rape or attempted rape during her college years.

And the women who make up half the US workforce of the twenty-first century? They make an average of seventy-eight cents to a man's dollar. That's higher than in the 1960s, but wage equality still remains out of reach. In 2014 women fill less than one-fifth of the seats in the US House of Representatives and Senate. Only 4.8 percent of chief executive officers (CEOs) of leading Fortune 500 companies are women. The ten top-paid Hollywood actors include Liam Neeson, Ben Affleck, Chris Hemsworth, Bradley Cooper . . . and not a single woman, not even Jennifer Lawrence. One exception to the rule? Oprah Winfrey. She's the only black female billionaire in all of North America.

Women work long days outside the home, but they still do the lion's share of domestic chores. Media images of superthin, sculpted female bodies create impossible beauty standards that drive many women to plastic surgery and to dangerous eating disorders. Honest and thorough sex education is not offered in many schools. In 2014 a boss could legally fire an employee for being gay in twenty-nine states and twenty-four states allow transgender workers to be fired for who they are too. Millions of LGBTQ people—those who identify as lesbian, gay, bisexual, transgender, queer, or questioning—face bullying, hate crimes, and police brutality.

Race intensifies these harsh realities. For example, the average Latina worker makes just fifty-four cents on a white man's dollar. Many women of color, who bear the brunt of poverty in the United States, don't have access to affordable, high-quality medical care, and they are paying the price with higher rates of heart disease and other health problems. A black woman in the United States is over three times more likely than a white woman to die during childbirth. Birth control and abortion are anything but miracles of feminism for women who want them but who can't afford them or who can't take time off work to go to a clinic a day's drive away.

Jobs in the United States are still gender-based. For example, most hotel housekeepers are women. The job is the most dangerous in the hotel industry, with an average injury rate of about 8 percent each year, twice the rate for all US workers. Risks include injuries related to repetitive tasks, such as pushing heavy linen carts and lifting heavy mattresses, as well as falling on the job, and in some cases, facing sexual assault from guests.

As a movement, feminism still has a lot of work left to do on issues of economic equality, sexual violence, and sexist media images of women. Its mission is expanding too to include issues of race and gender identity. In 1992 Rebecca Walker kicked off a new era of feminism with a *Ms.* magazine article, "Becoming the Third Wave." Feminism is more necessary than ever, she argued, and young feminists have carried that message into the twenty-first century.

THE F-WORD

"Are you a feminist?"

Polls show that this deceptively simple question hides countless complications. Depending on the polling source, between 23 to 68 percent of US women identify as feminists. Almost anyone, male or female, will say they believe in equal rights between men and women. But there's something about *feminism*—an American f-word—that makes the answer to "Are you a feminist?" complicated.

"Some people think that even uttering the word *feminism* is equivalent to saying, 'men suck,'" explains Anna Holmes, the founding editor of the feminist women's interest blog *Jezebel*. If women are in, men are out, the thinking goes. Pop singer Lady Gaga tapped into this sentiment when she said, "I'm not a feminist. I hail men! I love men!" (She later rethought this remark, saying that she did consider herself a feminist after all.)

Other women say that they don't believe feminism is necessary anymore and that they resent being treated as if they are victims. Some dismiss feminism as annoyingly politically correct, a movement that's simultaneously self-righteous and ridiculous. Still other women feel that feminism hasn't done enough to address issues of race and gender, while others can't get over the stereotype of feminists as stern women in sensible shoes who look down on makeup and other joys of femininity.

WHAT IS FEMINISM?

In the twenty-first century, feminists seem to be spending a lot of time explaining what feminism *isn't*. It's *not* about hating men or giving up lipstick or judging other women for the choices they make in their lives. Feminism is a huge, varied, and evolving movement. The heart of feminism has never been about undercutting men, creating fashion police, or shaming other women.

So what *is* feminism?

Most people start with the dictionary definition. Feminism is "the theory of political, economic, and social equality of the sexes," as well as "organized activity on behalf of women's rights and interests." In other words, feminism is both a set of ideas *and* action. It's an individual pursuit *and* it's a mass movement. Feminism takes place on multiple levels. It's political (a struggle for antidiscrimination laws and for rights of victims of rape and domestic violence). It's economic (a push for better wages for women). And it's social (an effort to raise awareness of women's lives through movies, history classes, and library collections). It's also very personal. Feminism empowers women to express their sexuality and their womanhood in their own way. Feminists know that TV shows such as *The Bachelor* don't have to be a template for the rest of us. They know that femininity can encompass everything from pink stockings to a hard hat.

Feminism trains women to notice when they are being unfairly ignored or passed over. It gets women asking themselves questions such as, "Why is he doing all the talking?" or "Why am I doing all the dishes?"

Pioneering American feminist bell hooks (the pen name of Gloria Jean Watkins) and the many who follow in her footsteps expand the definition of feminism even further. They feel that the dictionary describes only a reform movement. She and others are looking for a social revolution. For example, hooks points out that the societies in which women live in the twenty-first century oppress the poor and people of color. Female workers sew clothes in sweatshops all over the world, working for little pay and often in dangerous conditions. Immigrant mothers struggle to provide health care for their children. Nannies brought to the United States and Europe from poor nations of Africa and Asia work long hours for low pay. Many women and girls sell their bodies for sex to make a living. She and her supporters believe that the goal of feminism is to liberate *all* women from all forms of domination—and this will require societies to revolutionize how they work.

Another major goal of feminism, according to hooks and others, is to expose and eradicate sexism—the idea that masculinity, as traditionally embodied in strength, intellect, and control, is superior to femininity, which is traditionally perceived as weak, emotional, and submissive. Sexism also assigns stereotypical and distinct fashions, likes, dislikes, jobs, and activities to men and different ones to women. Sexism insists on clear boundaries between what is viewed as masculine and what is viewed as feminine. Sexism devalues women. But it also hurts men, by putting harsh limits on what is socially acceptable for them to do and in how they choose to express themselves. Cry in public? Wear pink every day? Probably not okay for a man. In a sexist world, a male who likes activities and fashions traditionally associated with feminine tastes will often automatically be assumed to be gay, even if he isn't, and perhaps ridiculed for those preferences. And girls who get into traditional male activities and fashions face the same assumptions and ridicule.

WHAT IS FEMINISM?

"It's not the decisions one makes so much as the ability to make a decision that indicates whether feminism has arrived in your life."
—Jennifer Baumgardner, *F'em! Goo Goo, Gaga, and Some Thoughts on Balls*, 2011

"Feminism is a philosophy that favors interdependence and cooperation over hierarchy and competition."
—Ani DiFranco, singer, 2011

"I myself have never been able to find out precisely what feminism is: I only know that people call me a feminist whenever I express sentiments that differentiate me from a doormat."

—Rebecca West, the *Clarion*, 1913

"Simply put, feminism is a movement to end sexism, sexist exploitation, and oppression."

—bell hooks, *Feminism Is for Everybody*, 2000

"Feminism is most essentially a way of thinking and acting in the world. By transforming our understanding of power relations in men and women's lives, feminism can teach us how to transform society itself so that both equality and liberation can be achieved."

—Rory Dicker, *A History of U.S. Feminisms*, 2008

"What is feminism? Simply the belief that women should be as free as men, however nuts, dim, deluded, badly dressed, fat, receding, lazy and smug they might be."

—Caitlin Moran *(right)*,
How to Be a Woman, 2012

SOME TYPES OF FEMINISM

» **antiporn feminism:** In the 1980s, feminists took sides in the so-called porn wars against the pornography industry and the magazines, movies, and other formats that show naked people engaging in sexual acts for the purpose of sexually stimulating viewers. Antipornography feminists wanted to do away with the X-rated industry because they felt it demeaned and dehumanized women. On the other side, pro-sex feminists defended sexual desire and free expression. The media helped give rise to the popular myth that feminists are antisex.

» **cultural feminism:** Women are essentially different from men, cultural feminists assert. They are more nurturing, cooperative, and communicative. Instead of measuring themselves against men, women should make their own activities more visible and valued.

» **Girlies:** These cultural feminists emphasize the value of pursuing domestic arts, fashion, makeup, and feminine sexiness.

» **hip-hop feminism:** A term coined by Joan Morgan in 2000, hip-hop feminism reflects a movement that focuses on the twenty-first-century black woman's experience. It rejects the victimization of women; embraces men; and like hip-hop music, celebrates overlapping, contradictory voices.

» **lesbian feminism:** This strain of feminism came together in the early 1970s and lasted through the 1980s, partly in response to homophobia within the mainstream movement. These feminists theorized that male domination and heterosexism work together to oppress women. Lesbian thinkers such as Adrienne Rich and Sheila Jeffreys viewed lesbianism as the logical extension of feminism—a conscious resistance to male domination.

» **queer feminism:** Unlike cultural feminists, queer feminists argue that nothing about gender is inborn. Gender is a social construct, or a performance we learn from birth. They view the gender binary—the idea of two and only two genders (masculine and feminine)—as a lie.

» **radical feminism:** Radical feminists aren't looking to share power with men. Radical feminists want to do away with all systems of power. These groups flourished in the late 1960s and early 1970s, and they still influence the movement of the twenty-first century, with a focus on fighting systems that oppress women and other minorities.

For many people, feminism starts with shedding their own internalized sexist ideas. This can be exhilarating. American feminists in the 1970s had a special word for each heady revelation about what they could be and how they could grow. It was described as a "click." As women revised their understanding of what they'd been taught was acceptable for a woman to want and be—often rejecting those limits—they came to a new and powerful awareness of their future potential, their strengths and weaknesses, their relationships, and their bodies. This new reality came into focus with a *click, click, click.* Feminism takes women out of the margins. It puts them in the center of history, politics, society, and their own lives. As writer Vivian Gornick put it, feminism is nothing less than "a profoundly new way of interpreting human experience."

CHAPTER ONE

THREE WAVES

OF FEMINISM

Chiefs, kings, composers, conquistadors, emperors, explorers, generals, men of letters, pharaohs, popes, scientists, inventors, sculptors, Vikings, Yogis, mythic gods . . . Name just about any contribution to human history, and one theme reigns: men dominate. For thousands of years, and in most cultures and eras, women have been viewed legally and socially as inferior beings. But there was a time, some twelve thousand years ago, when historians believe that men and women were likely considered equal in status. In ancient nomadic cultures, women mostly gathered fruits, berries, and other naturally growing seasonal foods and men mostly hunted game or fished local streams. Both men and women shared in rearing children, although women were primary caregivers during the time they breast-fed their babies. These roles weren't rigid, though. Women sometimes hunted, and men sometimes gathered. And one task was not valued more highly than the other. So what happened?

About 10,000 BCE, men and women settled down, literally. They abandoned their nomadic lifestyles and started living in homes and communities. Men and women divided tasks by gender. In this division of labor, women stayed at home to raise the children and do the work of the household. Women also cultivated crops. Men hunted, tended flocks, or

Women have contributed to human history in many undocumented ways. One goal of feminism has been to bring attention to these contributions and to foster a sense of accomplishment among women. For example, the Miss Cholita Paceña pageant in Bolivia seeks to foster pride in indigenous women of the Aymara and Quechua peoples, who are native to the Andes region of South America. This woman dances as part of her presentation at the pageant in 2007.

fished lakes and streams. Men and women began to form their own spheres, separate from each other.

Biological and Religious Roots

Men's and women's roles become more rigid, and soon enough, one came to be understood as superior to another. Biological differences between men and women provided an excellent justification for keeping women in their place. Women's bodies are outfitted for childbirth and nursing, and men are typically physically bigger and stronger than women. Even though most women in early agricultural societies performed backbreaking labor all day long, they came to be viewed as weak and inferior.

This sexism, fueled by biological facts, became encoded in law, culture, and religion. For example, in 1786 BCE, Babylon's leader Hammurabi devised the world's first set of written laws. Women were legally the property of their fathers, available for sale to potential husbands. The prized qualities of a bride—her virginity, most of all—became a woman's most valuable possession. In 384 BCE, the Greek thinker Aristotle added scientific heft to the prevailing gender scheme by "proving" that women were biologically inferior to men. His proof? Their "frigid" blood, which he said gave off less heat than men's. Moving into the Middle Ages (ca. 500 to 1500 CE), religious leaders such as Saint Thomas Aquinas added God to the argument. Women's roles had been preordained in heaven, he wrote. And on and on. Sexism became its own propelling force. By the nineteenth century, as women began to fight in earnest for their rights, they faced thousands of years of entrenched views about a woman's "natural" place in society.

ENTER FEMINISM

Not all societies in the world fell into this pattern of strict gender roles. As American Indian poet and critic Paula Gunn Allen has documented, North America's first feminist role models were the Indian women who held a great deal of power and respect in their tribes. For example, Iroquois and Cherokee clan mothers created war strategy and decided who among the tribe's male members would be the tribal chief. They developed herbal methods to control their fertility, and boys and girls were educated equally.

Most written histories about US feminism begin in the mid-nineteenth century, when the First Wave of three major waves of feminism began. Each wave describes, in very broad strokes, a historical and cultural era of feminism.

WAVE ONE: THE RIGHT TO VOTE

The First Wave spanned roughly 1848 to 1920. The struggles of the women's movement of those decades earned women the right to vote. First Wavers also won battles over women's rights to education, to own property, and to keep custody of their children after divorce. Suffragette leaders such as Elizabeth Cady Stanton, Lucretia Mott, Susan B. Anthony, and Sojourner Truth worked together to earn women the legal right to vote. (*Suffrage* refers to the right to vote in political elections.) Margaret Sanger, the founding mother of Planned Parenthood—an organization that promotes women's control over their reproduction—introduced the nation to the term *birth control* and is another First Wave icon.

The First Wave grew out of the abolitionist movement to end slavery in the United States. Abolitionist women agitated for the rights of black men, particularly the right to vote, and yet they didn't have these rights themselves. With this awareness, they started making speeches, writing books, holding protests, and taking a stand by voting illegally.

In 1848 the movement kicked off with the Seneca Falls Convention in New York. At this women's rights convention—the first in the nation—the Declaration of Sentiments and Resolutions captured the movement's goals. Elizabeth Cady Stanton was the primary author of this document—which she based on the American Declaration of Independence and revised to include women in the list of Americans who deserve liberty. The document's message spread across the United States, where it was met with general ridicule.

Elizabeth Cady Stanton *(far left)* was a key author of the Declaration of Sentiments and Resolutions. The declaration was presented in 1848 at the Seneca Falls Convention, the first women's rights convention in the United States. The document laid out a long list of grievances, including that women did not have the right to vote, own property, or pursue higher education. Stanton is seated in this photo from the 1890s with her longtime friend and feminist activist Susan B. Anthony. The two worked tirelessly for women's rights.

SO SELF-EVIDENT

The following is from the Declaration of Sentiments and Resolutions, a First Wave riff on the Declaration of Independence:

We hold these truths to be self-evident: that all men and women are created equal; that they are endowed by their Creator with certain inalienable rights; that among these are life, liberty, and the pursuit of happiness. . . . The history of mankind is a history of repeated injuries and usurpations [seizure of power] on the part of man toward woman, having in direct object the establishment of an absolute tyranny over her. To prove this, let facts be submitted to a candid world. He has never permitted her to exercise her inalienable right to the elective franchise [the vote]. He has compelled her to submit to laws, in the formation of which she had no voice. . . . He has taken from her all right in property, even to wages she earns. . . . In the covenant of marriage, she is compelled to promise obedience to her husband, he becoming, to all intents and purposes, her master—the law giving him power to deprive her of her liberty, and to administer chastisement [punishment]. . . . He closes against her all the avenues to wealth and distinction which he considers most honorable to himself. As a teacher of theology, medicine, or law, she is not known. He has denied her the facilities for obtaining a thorough education, all colleges being closed against her. . . . He has created a false public sentiment by giving to the world a different code of morals for men and women, by which moral delinquencies [failures] which exclude women from society, are not only tolerated, but deemed of little account in man. . . . He has endeavored, in every way that he could, to destroy her confidence in her own powers, to lessen her self-respect and to make her willing to lead a dependent and abject life.

So was Sojourner Truth, one of the first black women to take up the cause of feminism. In 1851 the former slave bared her breasts to a group of male hecklers at the Women's Rights Convention in Akron, Ohio. The exact words of Truth's speech are a matter of debate, but Truth is famously remembered for asking her audience again and again, "Ain't I a woman?" She was living proof that women were equal to men. After all, she'd done men's work all her life. "I have ploughed and planted, and gathered into barns, and no man could head me! And ain't I a woman? I could work as much and eat as much as a man—when—I could get it—and bear the lash as well!" she declared. Though it began in ridicule, Truth's speech is now considered one of the founding events of the women's movement.

FROM WAVE TO WAVE

First Wave feminist leaders introduced legislation to grant women the right to vote in every congressional session for forty-one years without success. Finally, on June 4, 1919, Congress passed the Nineteenth Amendment to the Constitution. It was ratified one year later, on August 18, 1920, and women's right to vote became law.

With this right, the First Wave began to ebb. Many Americans took the general view that the problems of feminism had been solved with women's participation in the ballot box. Even so, many First Wave activists, notably Alice Stokes Paul and her peers at the National Woman's Party, continued to push for total equality between men and women.

Suffragist Alice Stokes Paul raises a glass in the fall of 1920 to celebrate the passage of the Nineteenth Amendment to the US Constitution that August. The amendment, which became law that year, gave American women the right to vote. Paul also wrote and fought for an equal rights amendment to the Constitution. The amendment, though passed in both houses of Congress in 1972, has not been ratified by the states.

The Great Depression (1929–1942) hit Americans hard. During this period, about one-third of working Americans lost their jobs. As women and men scrambled to feed their families, concern for women's civil rights took a backseat. Then, on the heels of the Great Depression, the United States entered World War II (1939–1945). American soldiers joined the fight overseas, and American women filled factory jobs to manufacture war supplies.

With the end of the war, millions of soldiers came home to a booming American economy. They went to college and took over women's wage-earning jobs. Women were expected to be perfect housewives, devoting their lives selflessly to home and family. In truth, many housewives were bored and miserable. In 1963 Betty Friedan shattered the myth of the Happy Homemaker in her book *The Feminine Mystique,* which focused on the widespread unhappiness of American housewives. As Friedan's book flew off shelves, the Second Wave began to form.

In the coming decade, three forces came together to turn the Second Wave into a tsunami. One was the birth control pill. Developed in the 1950s, the Food and Drug Administration (FDA) approved the Pill in 1960. With this reliable contraceptive, women could, for the first time in history, plan their lives without having to take into account the interruption of regular pregnancies. At about this time, the US economy started to take a dive. Suddenly one man's income wasn't paying the family bills anymore and women reentered the workforce to supplement the household income.

The second and third forces were the civil rights and antiwar movements. These movements worked to bring racial justice to the United States and to end the nation's participation in the unpopular Vietnam War (1957–1975). Women signed on to both movements in large numbers, hoping to change the world for the better. Instead, they found themselves relegated to second-class status, acting as girlfriends, coffeemakers, and secretaries to the movements' male leaders. These ambitious women weren't satisfied with the backseat. They wanted more. So they turned their skills and efforts to address their own oppression.

WAVE TWO: FEMINISM EVERYWHERE

The Second Wave, from the late 1960s to the late 1980s, achieved victories in legalizing abortion, passing equal rights laws, and expanding sexual freedoms. Second Wavers rejected traditional notions of marriage and motherhood, urging women to pursue higher education and professional jobs outside the home. They made sexism an everyday word. They taught women to become more informed about and to take control of their own reproductive health and sex lives. Second Wave feminists made violence against women visible and identified it as a crime. They gave us the terms *date rape*, *sexual harassment*, and *domestic violence*. They set up domestic abuse shelters and rape crisis hotlines, and they fought for more comprehensive criminal justice. Second Wave pioneers introduced women's achievements into history textbooks and onto college reading lists. If First Wavers brought

OUR BODIES, OURSELVES

For many girls in the 1960s, getting their first period was an event clouded by shame, confusion, or even terror. Many had never been taught about menstruation, and they wondered what was happening to their bodies. These teen girls lived in an age when women's bodies and how they worked was a hushed topic and male doctors treated their female patients with a father-knows-best attitude. For girls and women, this meant "Don't ask questions." In 1971 a group of twelve feminists called the Boston Women's Health Book Collective published a guide to counteract these attitudes and to help educate women and girls about their bodies. *Our Bodies, Ourselves* offered frank information about women's health, sexuality, relationships, and even abortion (then illegal). The book became an instant feminist classic. Updated every four to six years, *Our Bodies, Ourselves* continues to be an important reference in women's health. As of 2014, it has been translated into twenty-nine languages and has sold more than four million copies.

feminism into the voting booth, Second Wavers brought it into courtrooms and capitols, workplaces, bedrooms, doctors' offices, schools, newspapers, and especially inside women's own heads.

Organizing began in 1966 when Betty Friedan, the Reverend Pauli Murray, and Shirley Chisholm founded the National Organization for Women (NOW). Along with small, leaderless liberation groups, NOW agitated for change through meetings and marches across the United States. Feminist thinkers such as Kate Millett, Alice Walker, Susan Brownmiller, Gloria Anzaldúa, and Audre Lorde examined race, violence, and sexuality through a feminist lens. They wrote classics, such as *Sexual Politics*, *Sister Outsider*, and *Against Our Will*, that women's studies majors are still reading on college campuses across the country.

Some historians point to the protests at the 1968 Miss America Pageant as another formative moment in the early history of the Second Wave of feminism. At the event in Atlantic City, New Jersey, about one hundred women marched up and down the boardwalk. They rallied against the contest, which they believed glorified oppressive beauty standards and judged women in the same way judges rank cattle at livestock competitions. "Welcome to the Miss America cattle auction," the protesters' signs read. "Let's judge ourselves as people." Protesters threw girdles, mops, pans, high heels, and other "instrument[s] of female torture" into a Freedom Trash Can. Reports later surfaced that the women had been planning to burn the contents of the trash can, and the myth of bra-burning feminists was born.

In living rooms across America, women were gathering in intimate consciousness-raising (CR) groups. As they told stories about unfair bosses or brutal boyfriends or sexual dissatisfaction, they began to understand that their common problems had roots in broader social systems. They coined the expression "The personal is political." This meant that private issues—such as sex and unwanted pregnancies, personal appearance and eating disorders, day care and the division of labor at home—were, in fact, societal problems with political solutions. Women encouraged one another not to blame themselves for these problems but to fight for equality in society and in the

Protesters gathered for a theatrical demonstration at the 1968 Miss America Pageant. The goal was to call attention to the event's inherent sexism and the way in which it degraded women as sex objects. The protest was one of the first media-savvy events to bring national attention to the emerging women's rights movement of the era.

nation's laws. Feminists Gloria Steinem and Dorothy Pitman Hughes launched *Ms.* magazine in 1972. The nation's first mass-circulation feminist magazine landed each month in women's mailboxes to continue the conversation.

BACKLASH

By the early 1970s, major splits had begun to develop within the feminist movement and a backlash began to surface. For instance, women of color and lesbians felt discounted. Some dropped out of the movement altogether, while others formed their own groups. Mainstream feminism had done little for many of these women, who had concerns that differed from those of the heterosexual, white, middle-class housewives at the core of the movement's leadership.

Feminist activists Gloria Steinem *(left)* and Dorothy Pitman Hughes *(right)* were among the cofounders of *Ms.* magazine in 1972. In this photo by Dan Wynn for *Esquire* magazine the year before, the women raise their fists in a power salute to show their shared feminist goals.

The issue of abortion also divided activists. While white women were fighting for the right to end pregnancies legally, women of color were fighting for the right to *become* pregnant. During the 1960s and 1970s—under the banner of a campaign against poverty—government-paid doctors coerced thousands of African American, Latina, and American Indian women to undergo medical sterilization so that they could not bear children. As a whole, the feminist movement ignored this practice of forced sterilization.

At this point in the evolution of the movement, some Americans felt that feminism seemed to have too many strict rules. To be a feminist, according to some perceptions of the movement, you had to actively rebel against traditional concepts of femininity. For example, some people felt that to be a good feminist meant that a woman couldn't shave her legs and that she couldn't wear a revealing bikini, high heels, or lipstick. A good feminist had to make sure a potential partner viewed her as an equal, not as a lightweight flirt, so flirting was a definite no-no. Second-wave feminism also pushed for changes to everyday language, so *girls* began to give way to *women*—sometimes spelled *womyn*—and *ladies* was out too. To some Americans, feminism felt antimale; antisex; anti-beauty; and most of all, anti-fun.

THE EQUAL RIGHTS AMENDMENT

Suffragist Alice Stokes Paul fought hard for women's right to vote, but she saw the Nineteenth Amendment as just a first step in a much larger struggle. Paul believed the women's movement required nothing less than a constitutional amendment guaranteeing equality between men and women. In 1923 Paul wrote a first draft of the Equal Rights Amendment (ERA). But passing a constitutional amendment is no small feat. It requires a two-thirds majority by both the US House of Representatives and the US Senate, plus ratification by at least three-fourths of the states. The ERA was introduced annually into every Congress from 1923 until 1972, when it finally cleared enough votes to be sent to the fifty states for ratification. Even then the amendment died when only thirty-five states—three states short—had signed up by a 1982 deadline.

What happened? Conservative opposition, famously led by an activist named Phyllis Schlafly, cast the ERA as pro-gay, pro-abortion, and antifamily. Inaccurate claims started spreading about the ERA: Men would be forced to work as strippers at clubs. Men and women would have to share public bathrooms. Women would lose their alimony and other divorce benefits. In the face of these claims, support for the ERA dwindled.

By the twenty-first century, a host of antidiscrimination laws protect women's rights at work and at school. For many Americans, the ERA just doesn't feel urgent anymore. ERA proponents argue that laws aren't enough—they can be overturned by a simple majority, and they often vary by state. The

Anti-ERA activist Phyllis Schlafly speaks at a rally at the state capitol in Springfield, Illinois, in 1978 to oppose the passage of the ERA amendment to the US Constitution. In the early 1970s, she founded the Eagle Forum to promote conservative issues and candidates. Since 1983 she has commented on a range of conservative causes through the *Phyllis Schlafly Report*, available on a daily basis, both in print and on radio stations around the country.

ERA would guarantee equal rights at the law's highest level, and it would be binding across the nation. All the same, the bill does not seem to have enough support to become a constitutional amendment.

Feminism also translated into a lot of work. For example, by the 1980s, the image of superwoman had replaced that of the Happy Homemaker as America's ideal female. The superwoman could do it all—have a high-paying, fulfilling professional job; run a perfect house; and raise darling children—except she couldn't. She was exhausted from bearing the brunt of work in the office and at home. Instead of blaming rigid bosses, slacker husbands, or structural problems such as unpaid maternity leave and limited day care, women blamed themselves. Feminism was making women miserable, or so the thinking went.

About this time, a rising conservative movement framed feminism as a threat to the traditional family and the American way of life. It pointed to feminism as the source of everything it deemed wrong with society. As conservative pundit Pat Robertson put it in 1992, feminism "[is] a socialist, anti-family political movement that encourages women to leave their husbands, kill their children, practice witchcraft, destroy capitalism, and become lesbians."

THE THIRD WAVE: EXPANDING DEFINITIONS

The Third Wave, which began in the early 1990s, was a reaction to the backlash and the weaknesses of the Second Wave. Young women, who had grown up with feminism in the water, realized they had benefited from Second Wave achievements and that they still needed the movement's wisdom. But they didn't feel at home in Second Wave feminism. Third Wavers wanted to carry on the movement's unfinished goals but with new tactics and a fresh perspective. In "Becoming the Third Wave," a 1992 article for *Ms.* magazine, Rebecca Walker (daughter of feminist author Alice Walker) wrote that she was done with conforming "to a way of living that doesn't allow for individuality, complexity, or less than perfect personal histories."

Walker and this wave of brash new feminists proclaimed themselves to be, among other things, pro-sex and pro-beauty. They were fun and in-your-face silly, reclaiming many derogatory or outdated words as feminist lingo. For example, the Third Wave reclaimed the word *girl*

Rebecca Walker is often credited with launching the Third Wave of American feminism through her 1992 article "Becoming the Third Wave" for *Ms.* magazine. She is the daughter of Pulitzer Prize–winning author Alice Walker and lawyer Mel Leventhal. Rebecca Walker writes about her life and identity in her autobiography *Black White and Jewish*, published in 2001.

with gusto. Guerrilla Girls had long been storming art galleries in gorilla masks, making a scene about the lack of female artists on museum walls. Meanwhile, Riot Grrrl revolted against sexism in the punk rock world. In bands such as Bikini Kill and Bratmobile, Riot Grrrl literally screamed about rape, incest, sexual double standards, and queer sexuality. Like the CR groups of the 1970s, Riot Grrrl groups began forming across the country to take up these issues in apartments and dorm rooms and eventually at conventions and conferences.

New feminist magazines such as *Bust* and *Bitch* took off in the mid-1990s with a wink and a smirk to offer their own take on pop culture topics such as beauty, language, books, fashion, and film. Do-it-yourself feminists created a flurry of zines—basically, stapled stacks of photocopies—that they mailed from living rooms or passed around college campuses. These low-budget magazines focused more on culture—what it meant to be a woman—than on political issues of the day. Writers shared their doubts and discoveries in first-person stories that were both shockingly intimate and extremely readable.

Guerrilla Girls formed in New York City in the mid-1980s to challenge racial and gender-based inequities in the arts world. They wore gorilla masks at their demonstrations and in their protest art to pull attention away from their individuality and toward their cause. The group is still active, and members take the names of dead female artists as pseudonyms. This poster from 2014 highlights how few women are represented in major US art museums.

In her 1995 song, "Hour Follows Hour," Ani DiFranco invented a fitting pun about the Third Wave: with every move, a woman made her own woman's movement. Third Wavers didn't have to earn their stripes as good feminists by going to marches and rallies. Standing up to a street harasser, encouraging children to freely express their gender, breaking sexist dress codes, blogging and tweeting about women's issues from an individual point of view—these all count as feminist activism in the Third Wave.

In 2000 Jennifer Baumgardner and Amy Richards published *Manifesta,* a manual for the Third Wave feminist movement. "Feminism wants you to be whoever you are—but with a political consciousness," they wrote. "And vice versa: you want to be a feminist to be exactly who you are." According to this Third Wave ethic, anyone could be a feminist, including housewives, men, sex workers, trans women, and other groups who had felt shunned by the Second Wave.

One of the most important goals of the Third Wave has been to widen the lens of feminism. Third Wavers expand their focus beyond gender to examine how other factors, including race, class, ability, age, and sexual orientation play out in women's lives. Academics have a word for this—*intersectionality.* They ask, for example, how sexual assault affects undocumented immigrant women, who fear being deported if they reach out to the police for help after being raped. Third Wave groups protest racist child protection policies that disproportionately remove troubled black children from their mothers while leaving troubled white children with their families. Or they look at police brutality in communities of color or how environmental toxins affect the safety of mothers' breast milk on Indian reservations. In the Third Wave, marginalized women and their communities have a spot in the center.

Some academics, journalists, and other writers—such as Ariel Levy, Camille Paglia, and Christina Hoff Sommers—have criticized the Third Wave as shallow, fragmented, apolitical, misguided, and ineffectual. Additionally, commentators such as Lisa Jervis, a founding editor and publisher of *Bitch* magazine, feel that the idea of a Third Wave sets up a false contrast to the Second Wave. She points out that the hallmarks of Third Wave feminism—from outlandish tactics to a focus on social justice—are abundant in Second Wave thinking. Jervis is uncomfortable with the very notion of feminist "waves," which she says creates a harmful and unjustified division within the larger, historical feminist movement.

A Third Waver might not necessarily disagree. She may not even know the term *Third Wave,* even as she's blogging about Hillary Clinton; making a princess costume for her son; volunteering at a girls' after-school program; lobbying her congresswoman; conducting a study on women's health; taking her son to a WNBA game; or crafting a subversive cross-stitch that says, "Bitches get stuff done."

CHAPTER TWO

EQUALITY

AT WORK

As the summer of 2014 began, Debra Harrell, a forty-six-year-old African American woman, faced a predicament shared by millions of other low-income, single mothers. What was she going to do for child care during the summer once school was out? She couldn't afford expensive summer camps, and she didn't have relatives available to help. Harrell's daughter, Regina, was nine and a half. She was old enough to keep herself busy on a laptop at McDonald's, where her mom worked.

During a break-in at the Harrell's house in North Augusta, South Carolina, the family's laptop was stolen. Bored to death at McDonald's, Regina asked her mom if she could hang out at the park by their house instead. Harrell said yes, figuring that the busy neighborhood park was safer than their own house, which had been burglarized twice in the past year. Harrell made sure Regina had a cell phone and a house key.

Regina spent several days on her own at the park. Sometimes she met up with friends. She ran on the splash pad or climbed on playground equipment. Volunteers distributed free breakfast and lunch on weekdays. Regina was never harmed. But at least a few local parents started to feel concern about her lack of supervision, and someone notified the authorities.

About 75 percent of mothers with children between the ages of six and seventeen participate in the US labor force. The statistic is about the same for single mothers with children under the age of eighteen. Many working mothers struggle to find consistent, affordable day care for their children while they are on the job.

On July 1, police arrested Debra Harrell for neglect of a child. As Debra headed to jail and social services took temporary custody of Regina, controversy erupted on airwaves across the nation. How could a mother be so irresponsible? some asked, shaking their heads. Others accused the government of overreaching its authority and worse. Would the police have stepped in if the Harrells had been wealthy, white people?

One local mother, Lesa Lamback, said: "I understand the mom may have been in a difficult situation not having someone to watch her child," she told a television reporter, "but at the same time, you've got to find somebody." Feminists, raised on the mantra of "The personal is political," looked at Harrell's dilemma as a symptom of larger social issues. Why was Harrell in this situation with her daughter in the first place? Why is child care so unaffordable? Why are Harrell's wages so low? Why are mothers overwhelmingly responsible for the care of children in the United States?

SEVENTY-EIGHT CENTS ON THE DOLLAR

Harrell's story struck a chord on issues of race, parenting, and low-income work. In particular, it shined a light on the intersecting issues of women's low-wage jobs and the hardships of single parenthood. Those two issues, in particular, drive an often quoted, poorly understood, and deeply controversial number: 78 percent. That's the gender wage gap in the United States.

Put another way, a full-time working woman in twenty-first-century America earns, on average, seventy-eight cents for every dollar earned by a full-time male worker. The wage gap gets even wider when you factor in race. For example, an African American woman typically earns sixty-four cents on a white man's dollar. According to the Institute for Women's Policy Research, the poverty rate for women as a group would be sliced in half if the wage gap closed up.

The gender wage gap varies further when age, job, education, and location are factored in. Still, it exists in every age group, every state, and almost every occupation. Even in female-dominated professions, such as nursing and teaching, men earn more. In addition, the gap has barely budged in a decade, even as women have outpaced men in all levels of higher education. What's going on?

WORKPLACE DISCRIMINATION

Lilly Ledbetter of Jacksonville, Alabama, had worked for nineteen years at a Goodyear Tire and Rubber assembly plant. Her salary was about 40 percent short of what men at her level were making. Though she was a supervisor, she earned less than the lowest-ranking man on the job.

Ledbetter found out about this wage discrimination in 2007 from an anonymous letter. But according to US law, she had only 180 days (about six months) from the first instance of discrimination—the first paycheck—to file a complaint. In other words, Ledbetter was eighteen years late in taking her case to court. Ledbetter decided to fight for her rights anyway, and her case went all the way to the US Supreme Court—where she lost in 2007. Democrats in the US House of Representatives quickly took action that year, drafting an anti-pay-discrimination bill that eventually passed in both houses of Congress and that President Barack Obama signed into law in January 2009. The historic Lilly Ledbetter Fair Pay Act restarts the 180-day limit every time a discriminatory paycheck is issued. Unfortunately for Ledbetter,

Lilly Ledbetter's long struggle for fair pay led to a new law in 2009 that loosens the time frame in which a woman can sue for wage discrimination. In this photo, she speaks at the 2012 Democratic National Convention in Charlotte, North Carolina.

the new law did not apply to her old case. She did not receive a single penny from her years of legal battles. However, Ledbetter is a prominent spokeswoman for workers' rights. In 2011 she was inducted into the National Women's Hall of Fame in New York City.

Ledbetter's case is extreme. Discrimination also works more subtly. Numerous studies have shown that employers are typically more impressed by male candidates, though not necessarily because of the candidate's qualifications. In one 2012 study at Yale University, employers were given fabricated résumés to fill a job as a lab manager on campus. The résumés were identical except that some had a female name at the top, and the others had a male name. The employers rated the female candidates as significantly less qualified than their fictional male peers. Even the female employers did so. Their reasoning did not include sexist language. They saw weaknesses in the "female" résumés that did not register when a male name was associated with it. So competing female candidates are pushed to the sidelines for jobs, promotions, and raises, more by deeply ingrained sexist habits than by outright malice. Race operates the same way—with employers favoring white job applicants—so women of color get hit twice as hard, despite antidiscrimination laws on the books.

Employers can take steps against this kind of subtle bias. In 1970 women comprised only 5 percent of musicians in the nation's top symphonies. To fix this, the orchestras auditioned candidates behind a screen, so the musician could be heard but not seen. By the mid-1990s, women filled five times as many orchestra seats—25 percent—thanks largely to the blind auditions.

Numerous studies have also documented the "double bind" that women face in the workplace, especially those in traditionally male positions. Women are scrutinized more than their male peers. They have to work harder to appear competent, but when they do take charge, they come across as unlikable.

To test the double bind, researchers have staged various scenarios in workplace environments. Hanna Rosin reports about a particularly telling situation in her 2012 book *The End of Men: And the Rise of Women.* In this test, a group of colleagues was getting ready to go to an office party when, all of a sudden, another coworker showed up in a panic. The copy machine was broken, he said, and he needed volunteers to help manually staple five hundred packets. The women who said no and went off to the party were later criticized viciously by the research subjects, while the men who said no were not judged at all. Gender stereotypes cast women as sacrificing and maternal, willing to help staple packets. Women who defy the role pay a price.

WOMEN'S WORK

Most experts agree that workplace discrimination in the twenty-first century is real, but it's just one, relatively small factor in the wage gap. Work is still extremely gendered in the United States, and traditional men's jobs—such as engineering and construction work—pay a lot more than traditional women's jobs, including nursing and education. Even though women earn three bachelor of arts degrees for every two earned by men, they flock to "female" fields that pay less than "male" jobs. Compare the median annual wage for a kindergarten teacher at $53,400 to a computer programmer's $74,280. Women's participation in high-paying STEM (science, technology, engineering, and math) jobs is extremely low. Women make up just 12 percent of engineers, for example. Meanwhile, they comprise more than 94 percent of housekeepers, nannies, and other domestic workers, which is about the lowest-paying, most undervalued work around. Women, disproportionately women of color, fill two-thirds of minimum-wage jobs in the United States. They are more than twice as likely as men to rely on tips—which are unpredictable and sometimes very low—for a living, a predicament that triples any worker's risk for falling into poverty.

Some people say that the gender gap is a myth and that women are freely choosing lower-paying jobs. After all, nobody is stopping a high school girl or college woman from going into STEM fields. But what if the thought never seriously entered her mind because she'd never seen an example of a female in the field? What if her parents told her she couldn't hack it? What if her mother told her, "Go ask Daddy to help you with your math homework" or her math teacher's gaze skipped right past her or she absorbed thousands of other subtle, cultural clues telling her science is unemotional, unimaginative, and unfeminine?

The number of women in the US science and engineering (S&E) labor force (which does not include all STEM fields, such as math) has stalled since about 2005 and is not much higher than it was in the 1990s. US women in the STEM fields tend to go into social sciences, math, or life sciences rather than computer science, architecture, and engineering, where they are generally outnumbered by men.

THE LEADERSHIP GAP

Women also aren't nabbing their share of the nation's most elite, high-paying jobs. Even though women just slightly outnumber men as mid-level managers, they're filling only about 15 percent of the seats in their companies' boardrooms.

Feminists used to call this phenomenon the glass ceiling. It's almost as if a woman gets trapped under an invisible ceiling as she climbs her way up the professional ladder. She can see the top but somehow can't reach it. In the twenty-first century, feminists have identified another, related barrier—they call it the maternal wall. This wall is extremely visible, with evidence pointing to it from every direction. Simply put, motherhood can be terrible for a woman's career.

First, take a look at the women who *are* at the top. They are overwhelmingly childless. The US Supreme Court offers a case in point. Every male Supreme Court justice has a wife and family. Of the three female justices, Ruth Bader Ginsburg began her career while her children were young. The other two female justices are single.

Sonia Sotomayor *(left, with President Barack Obama in 2009, after her appointment to the Supreme Court)* has served on the US Supreme Court since 2009. She is the court's third woman and first Latina. Her autobiography, *My Beloved World*, was published in 2013 and recounts her youth, education, and early career.

THE LANGUAGE GAP

As sociolinguist Jennifer Coates has documented in her book *Women, Men and Language*, women and men don't share equal rights on the conversational floor. Study after study shows that women talk less in mixed company. Men are more likely to interrupt women than the other way around. When women do take up equal discussion time, listeners often view them as pushy or overbearing.

Coates traces the language gap back to a woman's earliest days. Parents are more likely to use baby talk with female infants than with male infants, for example. Fathers and mothers are more likely to interrupt a daughter than a son. Analysis of classroom video footage shows that girls receive less of their teachers' "gaze" than boys. Although teachers look at girls less, this is not intentional, since teachers are surprised by the data.

Coates's book includes many transcripts of recorded classroom conversations. In one, kids are talking about how to determine the best president in US history. While boys blurt out answers, one girl is chastised for speaking out without raising her hand. Subtle messages like these add up over a woman's life to discourage her from participating on equal terms in conversation.

It's no wonder. Jobs at the top are incredibly demanding. They require long hours, travel, and rigid schedules, none of which mesh well with the demands of raising children. For two years, Anne-Marie Slaughter worked as the first woman director of policy planning at the US State Department in Washington, DC. "I never left the office early enough to go to any stores other than those open 24 hours," she writes, "which meant that everything from dry cleaning to hair appointments to Christmas shopping had to be done on weekends, amid children's sporting events, music lessons, family meals, and conference calls." Exhausted, Slaughter went back to her university job so she could spend more time with her teenage sons.

Scores of women don't even make it as far as Slaughter. As Facebook COO Sheryl Sandberg lamented in her controversial 2013 book, *Lean In*, women "opt out" as they become mothers. If they stay on the job, they cut back on their hours or reject promotions that would make more demands on their time. Many take a few years off or switch to part-time work while their children are young. At any given moment, about 23 percent of mothers are out of the paid workforce, while only 1 percent of fathers stay at home.

When a stay-at-home mother does return to the workforce, she may have a hard time finding a job. And if she finds one, her salary will take a hit, and it will never fully recover. A woman without children makes, on average, ninety cents or more to a man's dollar. That figure goes down once motherhood enters the picture. A working mother earns seventy-three cents to a man's dollar. For single mothers, the figure dips to sixty cents on a man's dollar.

THE POLITICAL GAP

Of the nation's one hundred US senators and 435 US representatives, fewer than one in five is a woman. And women make up only about one in ten of the nation's fifty governors and approximately nineteen thousand mayors.

When running for office, women in politics face more public scrutiny than their male opponents. Voters assume female candidates are less competent on matters of economic policy. According to a 2014 report by the nonpartisan Barbara Lee Family Foundation, voters trust women to fight for women's rights and view female candidates as peacemakers. In turn, voters don't like to see women going negative in attack ads. They tend to view this type of political behavior as unfeminine.

Nonetheless, women who run for political office are just as likely to win as their male opponents. However, women, especially young women, aren't running in equal numbers as men. In the 2013 report "Girls Just Wanna Not Run," researchers at American University in Washington, DC, identified five factors that keep young women from entering politics:

1. They're not brought up to think of themselves as political candidates.
2. They're exposed less to political discussions.
3. They care less about winning in general.
4. They are less encouraged to run by the people in their lives.
5. They underestimate their own abilities.

Organizations such as She Should Run work to encourage more women to get on the ballots. On the She Should Run website, you can nominate a woman who you think should run for office.

"Having a baby is the single worst financial decision an American woman can make," writes Ann Crittenden, author of *The Price of Motherhood*. In her book, she estimates that the "mommy tax" costs a typical college-educated mother $1 million in lost wages over her lifetime.

Behind the Maternal Wall

Many mothers in the US workforce value flexibility and fewer hours over high pay. In gendered US society, women still are seen—and see themselves—as the family caregiver. Meanwhile, men are praised for sacrificing their personal lives for work, which researchers suggest explains why fatherhood tends to boost a married man's career. As caregivers, women also simply have less time to put in at the office. On average, women spend twice as much time as men on household chores and taking care of kids because women carry primary responsibility for those tasks.

According to Kristin Rowe-Finkbeiner, cofounder of MomsRising.org, mothers also face their own brand of discrimination. Mothers who take time off, use flextime, and otherwise scramble to balance their family duties and careers are stigmatized as unreliable, unprofessional, or just too much trouble. A team of researchers at Cornell University in New York found that US mothers were 44 percent less likely to be hired than non-mothers with the same résumés. When mothers did land a corporate job, they were offered an average of $11,000 less in salary than a childless woman with the equivalent résumé.

Personal and Political Fixes

What's to be done? Two main approaches surface. One camp calls on individual women to close the so-called "ambition gap." Self-help-style books from these advocates, such as Sheryl Sandberg's *Lean In* and Katty Kay and Claire Shipman's *The Confidence Code* (2014), offer women tips for making it to the top. These books as well as corresponding workshops teach women to improve their negotiation skills. Women need to take more risks, stop being perfectionists, and value their own work more, these authors argue.

Mentoring programs also aim to help individual women and, especially, teen girls develop the skills and self-esteem they need to succeed. Organizations such as Girls Inc. and Young Women Rock! pair up girls and professional women for one-on-one outings. They offer after-school programs or summer camps, or they help arrange for internships and summer jobs. Some programs have shown remarkable success. Step Up Women's Network is a national group with fifty thousand supporters that focuses on underserved teen girls in urban areas. From 2010 to 2015, 100 percent of the high school seniors in their program have graduated and been accepted to college. Compare that to a 50 percent graduation rate for their peers who aren't in the program.

Even authors such as Sheryl Sandberg would agree, however, that self-help approaches can only do so much. Books like *Lean In*, especially, are aimed at career-oriented women and girls, not the millions, like Debra Harrell, who scrape out a living in low-wage jobs. And mentoring programs reach only a small percentage of those who need them. Still, some experts say that launching women into positions of power benefits all women. Women at the top serve as role models, and they are more likely than men to advocate for their sisters at the bottom. This controversial idea, pejoratively referred to as "trickle-down" feminism, is hard to prove, and the historical record to prove it works is up for grabs.

Lisa P. Jackson, former head of the Environmental Protection Agency, sums up the view of the second camp: "From my experience of breaking into a male-dominated field, I don't believe the solution is for women to simply inhabit a man's world. I believe we should make changes to that world." One high priority for making changes to that world is to raise the minimum wage. Experts estimate that raising the national minimum wage to $10.10 per hour would close up the gender pay gap by 5 percent in one fell swoop. The feminist wish list of change also includes programs to channel and encourage girls to move into high-paying STEM fields. American work culture needs to change too so that overall productivity is valued more than time at the office. In addition, workplaces need to offer flexible hours so employees can juggle work and home commitments. Studies show that a robust flextime policy is actually good for businesses, as it attracts talented employees and keeps job satisfaction high.

Another part of the change strategy is to tackle day care. In the United States, parents pay up to 50 percent of their salaries on day care. National paid sick time and family leave policies would provide a safety net to low-income parents who need to take time off to care for their families, while affordable day care would keep them out of poverty. As of 2014, the United States is just one of three countries that does not provide some kind of payment to new mothers who have taken maternity leave from their jobs. (The other two are Oman and Papua New Guinea.) Without paid leave, one-quarter of US women either quit or lose their jobs with the arrival of a baby, and 15 percent end up on public assistance. But as Rowe-Finkbeiner points out, paid leave for new fathers is just as important. How else are we going to change a culture that sidelines fathers and makes women the default caregivers in a family?

THE MOVIE GAP

The Bechdel Test offers an informal gauge of whether a movie passes a minimum threshold for including women. The test takes its name from the moviegoing policy of a character created in 1985 by lesbian feminist cartoonist Alison Bechdel in her comic strip *Dykes to Watch Out For*. The test asks this:

6. Does the movie have at least two female characters with names . . .
7. who speak to each other . . .
8. about something other than a man?

In a database of more than fifty-eight hundred movies at Bechdeltest.com, just 57 percent of movies pass the test. About 10 percent of movies fail all three criteria. According to a 2013 report, women fill only 30 percent of speaking roles in Hollywood movies and take the lead just 15 percent of the time.

CHAPTER THREE

VIOLENCE AGAINST WOMEN

On a May evening in 2014, Elliot Rodger went on a killing spree in Isla Vista, California. First, he stabbed three men to death in his apartment building. Then he drove his black BMW to the Alpha Phi sorority house at the University of California, Santa Barbara. He knocked on the door for two minutes. When no one answered, Rodger opened fire on three female pedestrians in front of the sorority.

Rodger then returned to his car. He drove around town, firing at pedestrians and running over cyclists. Within a short time, Rodger had killed six people and wounded thirteen. As police closed in on him, he shot himself in the head.

Rodger was mentally ill. Shortly before the murders and suicide, he had posted several disturbing YouTube videos. In one, he outlined his plans for a "day of retribution." He planned to seek revenge against all women who, he believed, had let him "rot in loneliness" and suffer the indignity of being a virgin at the age of twenty-two. He also directed his rage at the "obnoxious men" at whom girls threw themselves. His specific target was the Alpha Phi sorority house, where he said he would "slaughter every single spoiled, stuck-up, blond slut I see."

The reasons behind Rodger's murderous and suicidal violence are complex. On the one hand, some Americans pointed out that the mental health system had not been able to prevent Rodger's actions. Others called them a terrible consequence of gun culture. Feminists added another layer of explanation—misogyny, or the cultural hatred of women. Rodger grew up believing he was entitled to have his way with women. As an adult, he was active in so-called "men's rights" groups online, known for their particularly venomous comments about women. Rodger's parents had, in fact, contacted the police about his upsetting videos weeks before. Why didn't the police take action? Feminist writer Jessica Valenti explained that misogyny in young men is not a cause for alarm in US culture.

The tragedy surrounding Elliot Rodger touched a nerve. Soon thousands of American women were tweeting through #YesAllWomen about their own experiences of sexual violence, both directly and indirectly:

I am a rape and sexual assault survivor and my experience is not particularly unusual or rare. #YesAllWomen

[Violence against women is common] because we teach girls to dress decent instead of teaching boys to act decent. #YesAllWomen

#YesAllWomen learn to say "Sorry, I have a boyfriend" because we are only safe if we are another man's property.

[Rape is perpetuated] because society is more comfortable with people telling jokes about rape than it is with people revealing they've been raped. #YesAllWomen

Every single woman you know has been harassed. And just as importantly, every single woman you don't know has been harassed. #YesAllWomen

#YesAllWomen [Injustice prevails] because the media will mourn the lives of ruined high school football players, but not of the girls they assaulted.

I shouldn't have to hold my car keys in hand like a weapon & check over my shoulder every few seconds when I walk at night. #YesAllWomen

Rape and Domestic Violence

#YesAllWomen tapped into the pervasiveness of violence against women in the United States, including rape and domestic violence. The law defines rape as forced penetration in the vagina, anus, or mouth, though exact legal definitions vary from state to state. Rape hinges on consent—was the victim a willing partner? Was he or she even able to give consent? That's why sex with someone who is passed out, underage, or mentally disabled is often rape. Rape can happen inside a relationship too. One out of six American women has been the victim of rape or attempted rape. In most cases—about two-thirds of the time—a rape victim knows her attacker.

Domestic violence happens within any kind of intimate relationship. The partners can be straight or gay, married, unmarried, living together, or just dating. Often the beginning of the relationships starts out sweet. Then things just start to feel wrong. A boyfriend starts reading his girlfriend's texts without her permission. One partner pressures another to use drugs or alcohol. A husband keeps his wife away from her friends, he steals her money, or he threatens to harm her children or pets. Domestic abusers intimidate their partners through threats and isolation. In this context, physical violence becomes part of a larger pattern of behavior by one partner to control the other. One in four US women will experience domestic violence at some point during her life, with women in their early twenties most at risk.

An Ever-Widening Definition

Street harassment fits under the umbrella of violence against women too. Most women aren't flattered by strangers' unsolicited comments about their bodies as they walk to school or work, go for a jog, or take their kids to the park. In the feminist view, street harassment is a form of psychological violence that can carry the threat of rape. It's the menacing assertion that men control public spaces and that women in those spaces are objects to be appraised, corrected, or threatened. And it adds up. Any woman who has changed her way home from work, called a friend to say she got home safe,

EMPOWERING COMEBACKS

What should you do if someone catcalls you—keep walking or talk back? There's no right answer, and the decision often depends on circumstances. Are you in a dark alley alone? Or are you on a crowded sidewalk at lunch? How threatening is the person making the comments? Cards Against Street Harassment offers a creative option for those women who feel a response would be safe, who want to do something but who don't want to get into a full-blown confrontation. The website offers printable cards with straightforward messages to hand out to harassers.

» "Keep it to yourself."

» "Next time, just say hello."

» "It's not a compliment, and I don't like it."

or checked the backseat of her car before getting in has felt the cumulative effects of street harassment.

Female bloggers and gamers can attest to the heart-pounding seriousness of Internet threats too. Jessica Valenti, Amanda Hess, and other high-profile Internet feminist journalists have all faced rape threats pouring into their inboxes. In 2014 and 2015, feminist media critic Anita Sarkeesian and game developers Zoe Quinn and Brianna Wu were targeted by an online harassment effort. Known by its Twitter hashtag #gamergate, the harassers lashed out against the women's criticism of sexism in video games and of sexual harassment in the gaming world. The women faced rape threats, death threats, and the threat of releasing publicly shaming information about their personal lives. But the problem extends to all women who participate online. Early studies show that cyberbullying takes a gendered form. In one 2006 study, researchers at the University of Michigan set up a number of fake online accounts, some with usernames that seemed as if they would belong to women, others to men. Researchers then used the fake names to comment in chat rooms. The female-sounding usernames received some 100 sexually explicit or threatening messages a day. In comparison, masculine names got an average of only 3.7.

Sexual harassment in the workplace is another form of psychological violence, one that almost half of all working women have experienced firsthand. Sexual harassment comes in two main forms. In the first form, a woman's boss threatens to fire her if she doesn't perform sexual acts at his request. In the second scenario, a female worker puts up with so many lewd

STATE VIOLENCE

INCITE! is a radical feminist group that focuses on ending violence against women and transgender people of color. The group includes state crimes (violence and other crimes on the part of police, government, and other institutions of power) as part of the definition of violence against women. INCITE!'s website documents that poor women, trans women, and women of color are more likely to be the victims of invasive searches of their homes without a warrant, unfair arrests and false convictions, and excessive police force during an arrest.

Many state crimes against women of color stem from the so-called war on drugs, the federal government's efforts to stop the import, sale, manufacture, and use of illegal drugs in the United States. INCITE! argues that the war on drugs provides an excuse for racist government institutions to ignore the rights of people of color. For example, police illegally raid houses and search suspects in drug-ridden areas that are overwhelmingly in low-income communities of color.

Women of color are the fastest-growing group of people convicted of drug offenses. Women of color use drugs at comparable rates to white women, but various forms of oppression put them in the firing line. For one, women of color bear the brunt of poverty in the United States. About 25 percent of black, Latina, and American Indian women live in poverty—compared to 8 percent of white men and 10 percent of white women. That makes them more likely to turn to street economies, such as drug couriering (transporting drugs to sellers), to support their families. Women of color are also more likely to be trapped in abusive relationships, and some are forced to carry drugs for abusive partners. Mandatory minimum sentencing laws criminalize these low-level offenses, and the women end up serving big-time sentences for small-time crimes.

comments or demeaning remarks from coworkers, her workplace becomes unbearable and she quits her job.

What's the difference between sexual harassment and teasing or flirting? For one, sexual harassment is unwelcome, and it usually happens over and over again. On its website, the Feminist Majority Foundation lists dozens of examples of sexual harassment. Some of them are obvious, such as unwanted touching, stalking, or assault, but others are less so. These include leering, giving inappropriate gifts such as lingerie, pressuring for a date, "accidentally" brushing up against someone, addressing a woman with exaggerated or mocking "courtesy," displaying pornography at work, and obscene texts or phone calls. Many women may not realize they're being sexually harassed. They know they dread going to work—they call in sick when they're not, or they'd rather just quit than deal with a coworker who puts knots in their stomach. Sometimes they don't speak up because they worry their bosses will retaliate against them. They'll get the tasks nobody else wants, or they'll get their hours cut back.

Sexual harassment is illegal under federal law, and the US Equal Employment Opportunity Commission (EEOC) investigates hundreds of sexual harassment claims every year. But most cases don't get that far. Many businesses take it upon themselves to prevent sexual harassment with strict policies and workshops that teach workers about sexual harassment before it starts. In such companies, specially trained human resources (HR) staff resolve sexual harassment complaints as they come up.

PREDATORS AND PREY

Many people try to explain away an individual perpetrator's violent actions by saying the abuser must have been crazy, stressed out, strung out, or horny. Those circumstances may all be true, but most perpetrators don't rape, harass, or beat up their bosses, their teachers, or their coaches. They turn on someone less powerful in their lives—often a woman.

That's why feminists explain violence against women in terms of power. Rape, domestic abuse, and harassment are all forms of control over women, and they are perpetuated by a larger social system of sexism and misogyny that creates a rape culture. From her uniquely personal view on gender relations, trans woman Julia Serano puts a finer spin on it. She describes a predator-prey dynamic, where men are expected to act as aggressors and women as passive victims, objects, or onlookers. It's why women's bodies are treated like props to sell everything from beer to shoes to cologne. It's why phrases like "ballsy" and "man up" are synonymous with showing power or seizing what you want. And the dynamic cuts both ways. It's also why a teen boy who has sex with a woman is often viewed not as a victim but as "lucky" and why lone adult men get fearful sideways glances at playgrounds.

In the theory of rape culture, sexist and misogynistic social attitudes cause rape and perpetuate it too. Sexual assault is ignored, accepted, excused, denied, or blamed on the victim. One of the main efforts of Third Wave feminism is to debunk myths about rape, including the following:

- Rape is a natural behavior for men. (Most men aren't rapists.)
- Rape can be sexy. (Rape is terrifying and painful and can cause lasting psychological harm.)
- It's only rape if a woman physically fights back against a sexual encounter. (Rape involves any sexual encounter in which a woman does not give her consent, regardless of whether she fights back or not.)
- Men are often falsely accused of rape. (Most victims of rape are telling the truth when they report the crime. Studies report that only between 2 and 8 percent of sexual assault reports each year are false claims. They tend to be the result of a variety of reasons such as pressure to drop charges or trying to cover up an embarrassing sexual encounter.)
- When a woman says no to sex, she actually means yes. (*No* is a word that always indicates a person does not agree to participate in or with something.)

WHAT WERE YOU WEARING?

"Boys will be boys," is a common expression to excuse male sexual violence. At the same time, those boys' sisters are taught to pay close attention to what they wear, to stick together, and to stay out of *that* neighborhood. This well-meaning advice sets the stage for victim-blaming. The message to girls is, "If you get sexually attacked, it's your fault because you wore that tight dress," while boys learn that rape is OK because women were "asking for it."

Hip-hop feminist Latoya Peterson sums up attitudes from her own childhood: "If you were alone with a boy, you were asking for whatever he did to you. If you were raped at a party, you were asked why you chose to go in the first place. If a man followed you down the street, the question became, 'What were you wearing?'"

Victim-blaming happens in cases of domestic violence too. When a woman—especially a sex worker, a drug addict, or a transgender woman—is beaten up by her pimp, supplier, or male partner, many people

SLUTWALK

Second Wavers protested violence against women with solemn, candlelit Take Back the Night marches. A new generation of feminists did it with the SlutWalk, where protesters dressed up in fishnets and stilettos to thumb their noses at the patriarchy—a social structure that perpetuates male domination. The first SlutWalk took place in Toronto, Ontario, on April 3, 2011. The protest has gone on to become an annual event around the world. Protesters call for an end to rape culture and to linking women's appearance and clothing choices to rape. With their flashy protests, SlutWalk participants declare their freedom to wear whatever they want in public. To be a slut no longer implies "bad" sexual behavior but, instead, refers to a woman's control of her own sexuality.

ask, "What did she expect?" or "Why didn't she leave?" or "How could she go back to him?" In fact, leaving might seem like the worst of several bad options for an abused woman, who is trapped by her financial dependence on her abuser. She also has good reason to fear retaliation if she leaves, because leaving an abusive relationship actually increases an abused woman's chances of being killed by her partner. Feminists point out that the real question should be, "Why didn't *he* make a different choice?"

In a victim-blaming culture, most women don't report violence, and even when they do report it, perpetrators often go free. The numbers are especially startling when it comes to rape. In the United States, about 60 percent of rapes go unreported. When charges are brought, rapists spend time behind bars in only 2 to 3 percent of cases.

THE MOST VULNERABLE

Women have dozens of reasons for not reporting violent attacks. They blame themselves for the assault; the process of reporting and speaking to authorities is too frightening, embarrassing, and potentially assaultive; or they just want to move on with their lives. But for some women, the stakes are even higher. A poor woman trapped in an abusive relationship is often reluctant to report the violence because she may depend on her abuser for housing and for money to pay for food, child care, and other essentials. In 62 percent of the cases in which female soldiers report sexual assault, they face some form of retaliation, such as a demotion or loss in pay. Lesbians or trans women often fear being outed or abused by police. For an undocumented immigrant woman, the obstacles to feeling safe about reporting an assault are staggering. She may not speak English or understand the US legal system. She likely fears deportation or being scorned by friends and family.

For victims of human trafficking—forced illegally into sex work, agricultural labor, or domestic service by bosses and pimps who take most or all of their earnings—the obstacles are even worse. These women face violent, often deadly, retribution by their bosses and pimps if they go public

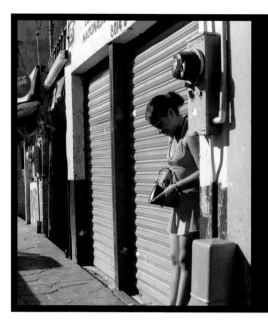

The sexual exploitation of children, especially females, is a lucrative—and illegal—international industry. Pimps and traffickers typically exploit children, such as this teen girl in Tijuana, Mexico, through street prostitution. They are also victimized in night clubs, illegal brothels, sex parties, motel rooms, hotel rooms, and other locations around the globe.

with the hardships of their lives. Like undocumented workers, they often do not speak English and do not know where to go or whom to ask for help.

American Indian women have seen violence on their reservations reach epidemic proportions, with one out of three women facing rape in her lifetime. An Alaska Native or American Indian woman is 2.5 times more likely to be sexually assaulted than other American women, and yet, for decades, she has had little recourse.

American Indian women have been trapped in a legal system that has completely failed them. Until 2015 the tribal government of an American Indian woman attacked by a non-Indian man on her reservation had no power to arrest, investigate, prosecute, or condemn her attacker. The woman's only recourse was to seek help from federal or state authorities in police stations and courthouses off the reservation. If an Indian woman did report her attack, her case might lag for years.

And in fact, American Indian women are attacked by non-Indian men in 86 percent of cases. (In other groups, most victims are raped by members of their same racial or ethnic community.) The attacks on Indian women are also generally more physically violent, leaving more bruises and other signs of struggle. Such facts suggest a bone-chilling trend. American Indian women are targets for sexual predators. Violent men have sought them out because they are so unprotected.

But vital change is taking place. In March 2015, tribal communities celebrated new landmark legislation aimed to protect Indian women. The Violence Against Women Act allows tribal governments to prosecute non-Indian men, and tribal governments are gradually figuring out how to enforce their new authority.

SEX WORK—IT'S COMPLICATED

Sex work is a broad term that includes jobs ranging from street sex workers to strippers to porn stars. For decades feminists have debated whether sex work is a form of violence against women. Those in the yes camp have argued that sex work objectifies and dehumanizes women and that it should be outlawed. The other side blames a societal double standard that celebrates male sexuality while repressing the same behavior in women. In their view, sex workers are shamed and criminalized for expressing female sexuality and their work should be legalized and respected.

A third camp of feminists takes a nuanced view. They recognize that sex work is extremely dangerous. Prostituted women, especially, are at high risk for sexually transmitted diseases and rape and beatings by clients, pimps, and police alike. Many women are forced into sex work by desperate circumstances, such as poverty or drug addiction. An alarming 80 percent of prostituted women started before the age of eighteen. But many sex workers don't want to be viewed as victims, and a minority find their work empowering and lucrative.

Many advocacy groups, including the Sex Workers Project, take a practical, "harm-reduction" approach. They assess an individual sex worker's needs, providing counseling, legal help, or health care without judgment. Other groups, such as the Polaris Project, continue to work at the policy level. One major goal is to decriminalize sex work by minors. Safe harbor laws treat underage prostitutes as victims of abuse, offering them protection and support instead of punishment.

CRISIS ON CAMPUS

Campus rapes are reported at low rates as well, even though the incidence of rape at colleges and universities is high. Research shows that one out of four women in the United States is sexually assaulted during her college years. Usually alcohol is involved. Experts used to describe campus rape as a type of date rape, a drunk hookup that goes awry. But recent studies have led to a new, more sinister understanding. Nine out of ten campus rapes are by repeat offenders. These serial rapists are seeking out vulnerable women, and young college women are an easy target. Instead of a gun or a fist, rapists use alcohol to subdue their victims.

Less than 5 percent of campus rapes are reported, and college men found guilty of sexual assault are rarely expelled. Often these cases become a matter of "he said/she said"—one person's word against another. These cases are hard to prove. Additionally, college leaders tend to sweep campus rape under the rug because it hurts fund-raising and can harm a school's reputation.

Emma Sulkowicz, a Columbia University visual arts student, claimed she had been raped in her dorm room in 2012. In response to the rape, she created a senior thesis protest project called "Mattress Performance (Carry That Weight)" in which she carried her mattress *(left)* with her everywhere she went on campus, with the goal of ending her protest when her alleged rapist was either expelled or left the university. Lacking sufficient evidence, officials did not pursue criminal charges against the student. Sulkowicz ended her protest when she graduated in the spring of 2015. Several female friends helped her carry her mattress to the graduation ceremony.

Feminist activists are fighting back in the courts, relying on the landmark 1972 Title IX law that bans federally funded colleges from gender discrimination. In 2014 more than fifty-five colleges were under investigation for failure to handle sexual assault cases under Title IX. Meanwhile, an approach known as bystander education is proving to be one of the most effective antirape strategies on campus. Bystander education teaches friends to look out for one another at parties, where drinking can put people at a higher risk for sexual assault. Through role-playing and workshops, students learn to recognize the danger signs of excessive drinking and sexual harassment and how to speak up and defend one another when they see it.

Yes Means Yes!

For decades, feminists looked at the issue of sexual consent from a "No means no!" perspective. This empowering slogan affirmed a woman's right to lay out sexual boundaries. It also spread the message that a woman's wishes about her body were nonnegotiable. One goal of Third Wave feminists is to update the issue of sexual consent. In a courtroom setting, "No means no!" can be problematic. It could imply that rapists should not be found guilty because a victim did not say no to the sex act. In many cases, victims of rape do not say no because they are too shocked, scared, or drunk to even speak. In the twenty-first century, Third Wave feminists are arguing for affirmative consent in sexual relations. This "Yes means yes!" approach to sex means that both partners must actively agree to sex for it to be truly consensual. In the absence of a spoken yes, the sex act can be legally viewed as unwanted, nonconsensual sex—rape.

"Yes means yes!" protects against what Latoya Peterson calls "not-rape," demeaning sexual situations that made her and her friends feel powerless growing up: "Being pressured into losing your virginity in a swimming pool pump room to keep your older boyfriend happy; waking up at night to find a trusted family friend in bed with you; having your mother's boyfriend ask you for sexual favors; feeling the same boys grope you between classes, day after day."

"Yes means yes!" also changes the tone of the wider societal conversation about sexuality. "No means no!" casts women as prudes whose job in the bedroom is to put on the brakes. "Yes means yes!" acknowledges that women are sexual equals to men.

"DON'T RAPE!"

Third Wave feminists are changing the cultural message from "Don't get raped" to "Don't rape." Jennifer Baumgardner is tired of signs like this one in a New York subway: "You don't have to accept sexual harassment. Say No! Report It!" She offers a feminist revision: "Don't abuse or sexually harass anyone! If you do, you are disgusting and will be punished!" Male feminists, such as those in Men Can Stop Rape, are developing programs that teach men how to create healthy, equitable relationships that don't rely on dominance and power.

The feminists at INCITE! sharply criticize the methods of the mainstream antiviolence movement. In their view, mainstream feminists have come to rely almost exclusively on the criminal justice system—police, courts, and prisons—to solve issues of violence against women. By doing so, these women's groups are actually strengthening what INCITE! and other radical feminists view as dangerous institutions. As radical feminist Angela Davis puts it, "Can a state that is so thoroughly infused with racism, male dominance, class bias, and homophobia . . . minimize violence in the lives of women?" She said that the criminal justice system has done little to keep women safe and that it has created only the illusion of safety.

These radical women encourage other feminists to keep widening their net of action, to go beyond law-and-order agendas. Humane immigration policy, prison reform, strong tribal governments, and economic justice—*these* are among the goals that will end violence against women at its roots.

CHAPTER FOUR

SEX AND BEAUTY

Rebel is maybe not the first word that comes to mind when you think of *American Idol* winner Kelly Clarkson. But in 2009, the pop star defied society's standards for women in a shocking way. She didn't star in a sex video. She didn't join a cult or shave her head. So what did Clarkson do?

She gained weight. And, unlike Oprah Winfrey, Tyra Banks, and dozens of other stars who have found themselves in her condition, Clarkson didn't apologize. She kept wearing fitted tops and curve-hugging skirts. In 2009 Clarkson appeared on the cover of *Self* magazine's 2009 "Total Body Confidence Issue" with this message:

> *My happy weight changes. . . . Sometimes I eat more; sometimes I play more. I'll be different sizes all the time. When people talk about my weight, I'm like, "You seem to have a problem with it; I don't. I'm fine!" I've never felt uncomfortable on the red carpet or anything.*

But there's a twist to this happy ending. *Self*'s smiling, windblown image of Clarkson wasn't quite right. Her arms were weirdly cropped. She had a big yellow dot covering her rear. Most of all, Clarkson was looking at least two dress sizes smaller than she was in real life. The writers at *Jezebel* and other feminist sites called out the gaffe immediately. *Self* had photoshopped

Female celebrities, such as Kelly Clarkson *(left, performing on* Good Morning America *in 2009),* face tremendous pressure to stay thin. If they gain weight, magazines and other media typically alter images to make the women look thinner.

Clarkson to what it viewed as an acceptable size. The magazine's editors defended their decision, claiming they were simply following industry practices to make women look thinner. On her personal blog, *Self* editor in chief Lucy Danziger went a step further. The magazine had done Clarkson a favor by showing the singer's "personal best," Danziger remarked.

The irony was not lost on feminists: A woman's "personal best" equaled a *fake* representation of her. The beauty cult had eaten up and swallowed the real Kelly Clarkson.

BEAUTY CULT

Imagine a world where girls don't obsess about their hair and women don't lose sleep about wrinkles. Imagine that women and girls are happy with the shapes and sizes of their bodies. Imagine that movies and media reflect a dazzling array of ethnicities, physiques, and abilities—even in sex scenes. *Fat* is just a physical descriptor, like blond or tall, that people don't take to mean *gross, embarrassing, lazy,* or *bad.* In this world, a woman's looks aren't constantly scrutinized, appraised, and compared to other women's looks. A female politician's hairdo isn't news, and nobody notices if she wears the same outfit twice in one month.

DATA DUMP

» The average American woman uses ten beauty products every day.

» Only 5 percent of US women are as naturally thin as models.

» From 40 to 60 percent of girls aged six to twelve are concerned about their weight.

» Women make up nine out of every ten patients on a cosmetic surgeon's table.

» About 85 percent of people who buy weight-loss products and services are women.

What's happening in this feminist dream world? The beauty cult, which feminists also call the beauty myth, or the beauty construct, has gone extinct. Beauty is still valued, but it's not the key to being a powerful, respected female. It's not so narrowly defined as to marginalize and humiliate or shame most real women. Even more, it's not an obsession that comes at the expense of other forms of female power.

A GROWING GAP

Author and filmmaker Jean Kilbourne has been studying images of women in American media since the late 1960s. Back then she was disturbed by the way companies used only images of thin, conventionally beautiful (most often white) women to sell everything from cars to beer to cigarettes. The women in the ads were objectified. They were treated like stage props, without feelings, personality, intelligence, or a point of view. Often only certain parts of their bodies—breasts, hips, and legs—were featured in the ads. All the women were completely interchangeable.

Over the decades, Kilbourne has seen American consumer culture explode. Add in the expansion of cable and online media outlets, and viewers are blitzed with hundreds of images of objectified female beauty every day.

And that beauty ideal is getting narrower and narrower—literally. Female models, pop stars, and celebrities are thinner than ever. Through digital enhancing, their hair is more perfect, their skin is more flawless, their thighs and waists are smaller, and their breasts are bigger. The beauty standard has become impossible—and dangerous—for ordinary women to emulate. As Kilbourne puts it, even supermodels need to be photoshopped to look like supermodels.

Meanwhile, the size of the average American woman is getting larger. While most models are a size 0 or a size 2, the average US woman is a size 14. Also, while images of women of color in ads are more prevalent than they were in the 1970s, white beauty standards, such as smooth hair and round eyes, still reign. The gap between idealized beauty and reality is wider than it's ever been.

Logos featuring female characters have become thinner over time. For example, Miss Columbia (also known as Lady Columbia) of Columbia Pictures had a curvaceous figure in the film studio's 1940 logo *(left)*. By the twenty-first century, she had lost her curves in favor of a slimmer, boyish figure *(right)*.

Beauty Sickness

Women know about the beauty gap, says feminist psychologist Renee Engeln. Nonetheless, the beauty ideal is so deeply embedded in women's worldview that they still cave to the pressure of impossible beauty standards. She calls the phenomenon "beauty sickness."

In a culture sick with beauty, women feel that their bodies are always being observed—and that those bodies are imperfect. It's as if a mirror follows them wherever they go. Engeln calls this "self-objectification"—women treat themselves as beauty objects. And so a woman checks her lipstick in her rearview mirror while she's driving. "How's my hair?" another asks her friend. Teen girls gather in the bathroom to compare how their butts look in their jeans.

And what's wrong with that, exactly? For one, it leads to low self-esteem, poor body image, and depression. But even discounting those factors, it's a huge distraction. How can a young woman—anybody—concentrate on

FAT HATRED

Fat is a word to describe the relative amount of adipose tissue in a body. But in US culture, fat is cast in moral terms. If you stick to your diet? You've been *good*. If you eat too much? You *cheated*. Few stereotypes are as widely accepted as the fat person who's lazy, out of control, or gross.

Fat hatred affects women more viciously than men. According to a 2011 study, a woman who packs 25 extra pounds (11 kilograms) is more likely to be skipped over for promotions and to lose out on job opportunities. She earns an average of $13,847 less a year than her thinner counterparts. Very thin women earn on average $15,572 more each year than average-sized women. As for men, their chances of climbing the corporate ladder actually improve with added body weight.

NO OFFENSE TO OPRAH

"I have read more about Oprah Winfrey's ass than I have about the rise of China as an economic superpower. I fear this is no exaggeration. Perhaps China is rising as an economic superpower because its women aren't spending all their time reading about Oprah Winfrey's ass."

—Caitlin Moran, *How to Be a Woman*, 2011

high-level calculus, studying voice and music, philosophical quandaries, or subtle poetry mechanics if she's worried about how she looks? Add in the accompanying expense, pain, or both of cosmetics, diet programs, and plastic surgery, and the burden can be staggering. In her Third Wave classic, *The Beauty Myth*, Naomi Wolf called the beauty cult nothing less than "a political weapon against women's advancement."

DANGEROUS CONSEQUENCES

The consequences don't end there. Feminists have long connected objectification of women with epidemic rates of sexual violence against women. Objectified images don't necessarily trigger violence, but they create a dangerous climate. As Jean Kilbourne says, "Turning a human being into a thing is almost always the first step toward justifying violence against that person." So, even though ads also objectify male bodies (though far less often), the images don't carry the same sinister undertones. As a group, men have more power in society and don't live under the threat of sexual assault the way women do.

Men and boys are also about ten times less likely than women and girls to develop anorexia and bulimia. Eating disorders have steadily been on the

FIVE CURES FOR BEAUTY SICKNESS

Feminists are working against the beauty cult from all sides. They put pressure on the fashion industry and on advertising companies to change media images to reflect the way real women look. Some companies seem to be taking the issue to heart. In 2014 Dove celebrated ten years of its "Real Beauty" advertising campaign, which features regular women in ads. Some companies, including American Eagle, have taken pledges not to photoshop their models. Feminists also teach strategies for women and girls to feel good in their own skin. Here are five tactics to resist the beauty cult:

1. Support media that does not objectify women.
2. Think of your body as a whole, not just a bunch of parts.
3. Focus on what your body can do, instead of how it looks.
4. Limit mirror time.
5. Don't tell little girls only how pretty they are. Find other ways to compliment them.

rise since the 1950s and can be deadly. These disorders are complex, and there's not one clear set of causes. However, researchers agree that cultural standards that glorify thinness can exacerbate an existing problem.

Abra Fortune Chernik struggled with anorexia for more than two years, including three months of hospitalization. She has written eloquently about how society's fetish for thinness played a role in her illness. One day she went to the mall and had her body fat tested at a fitness store. When the result came back at just 10 percent body fat, the man who had tested her offered his congratulations: "The average for a woman your age is twenty-five percent," he told her. "You're this week's blue ribbon winner!"

A few weeks later, Chernik had reached a turning point in her recovery. She realized that her eating disorder was more than just a personal trauma:

Gazing in the mirror at my emaciated body, I observed a woman held up by her culture as the physical ideal because she was starving, self-obsessed and powerless, a woman called beautiful because she threatened no one except herself.

PORN CULTURE

In 1983 Hasbro toy company introduced an adorable pony doll for girls. This plastic pony had long, silky hair and big eyes with eyelashes. It had freckles and "cutie marks," such as bows, on its haunches. My Little Pony was about as girly as you could get.

Fast-forward thirty-plus years, and My Little Pony has gone from girly to sexy. The pony's gotten thinner, with a pronounced waist and a curved chest. Her eyes are bigger, and her hair is longer. In 2013 Hasbro introduced a half-human version of Pony called Equestria Girl. She prances around in knee-high lace-up boots.

Toys for girls are increasingly sexualized. For example, Hasbro's My Little Pony has become thinner and gained longer, curlier hair; pouty lips; and bigger eyes *(above)*. Her body language is generally far more

My Little Pony's makeover is just one telling symptom of what feminists call porn culture. In this cultural climate, Target and other stores sell padded bras for girls as young as six, and activists fight to take thong underwear for preteen girls off the shelves at Abercrombie & Fitch. Parents have also spoken out about Victoria's Secret line for teens, called Pink. It features lacy, see-through training bras and T-shirts with scrawling messages that say, "Enjoy the view," and "Take me to paradise." Women sign up for cardio striptease classes at their local gyms, and Olympic

BLACK BODIES

American culture oversexualizes female bodies, particularly those of black women. The image of the wild black sexual temptress is sometimes called a Jezebel, after one of the Bible's most reviled female characters. The black temptress is a historical stereotype that is common even in modern hip-hop videos and other media images. Some feminists view Nicki Minaj's "Anaconda"

video, with its close-up shots of the artist's thrusting hips and buttocks and other highly sexualized imagery, as a typical example. Minaj herself, however, says of the video, "It's always about the female taking back the power, and if you want to be flirty and funny that's fine, but always keeping the power and the control in everything."

athletes pose naked for *Playboy*. Screens everywhere flash with scantily clad women writhing, groaning, moaning, thrusting, and licking their lips for the camera.

As with the beauty cult, porn culture focuses mostly on women and girls. Women's bodies are eroticized, over and over again. And the repeat performances are targeted for the exclusive arousal of heterosexual men. Like beauty, porn culture "sexy" is limiting, unrealistic, and unachievable. Worst of all, it's interfering with girls' healthy sexual development.

The Jezebel stereotype goes back to the days of slavery, when white masters routinely raped black female slaves. Viewing a black woman as a sexual savage was one way to justify the white master's crime. That way the blame for the crime was on her not him. He couldn't be expected to resist such temptation. This thinking also allowed white women to blame their slaves instead of their husbands for their cheating. Over time, a harmful contrast arose in the culture. The oversexed black woman served as an opposite to her virtuous white counterpart. So the false image of the sex-crazed black woman made white women look good by comparison.

A classic example of the stereotyped depiction of black women was the so-called Hottentot Venus (Saartjie Baartman), a woman from southern Africa with what were perceived by Europeans as large buttocks. She was on exhibit in western Europe in the early 1800s as an exotic species. The French engraving of Baartman *(right)* dates to about 1814.

In 2015 Madame Tussaud's wax museum in Las Vegas added a wax figure of Minaj *(left)*, based on the "Anaconda" video, one of the most popular of 2014. Some feminists view Minaj's image as a modern Jezebel stereotype.

La Venus Hottentote.

Porn and Purity

In porn culture, young women give up control of their own sexuality. Instead of learning about their own bodies and their own desire, they learn how to become desired objects. While teen boys ask themselves, "What do I want?" teen girls wonder, "Am I hot enough?"

"Hot" is an appealing source of power, even if it's hard to pin down. *Hot* means looking the right way, wearing the right clothes, and showing the right kinds of moves. Feminists point out that for young women, whose own sexuality is still forming, *hot* means mimicking what they see around them. For them, female sexuality is therefore about performance, not pleasure.

Feminists also believe that porn culture is especially harmful when girls, boys, and teens don't have access to informative, fact-based sex education. In porn culture, girls who look physically ready for sex but are far from it are at a higher risk of giving in to pressures to have sex but without any savvy about the risks. Solid information about sex and human reproduction can help girls and boys make healthy, safe choices about their bodies and resist the sexualized messages of porn culture.

While American girls are being bombarded with messages about how to be hot, about 16 percent of girls are signing up for the virginity movement. At church or chastity events, girls as young as six sign cards promising not to have sex before marriage. They wear special rings to seal their promise. At purity balls, girls get dressed up in prom dresses to pledge their sexual purity on the arms of their tuxedoed fathers in candlelit ceremonies.

However, research shows that the vast majority of pledgers break their promise, and when they do, they're significantly less likely to practice safe sex. And they engage in sex behaviors that don't technically break the (heterosexually defined) virginity threshold but are still risky. So rates of sexually transmitted infections (STIs) are higher among this group.

From a feminist point of view, the purity movement fits right into porn culture. Once again, girls are being told that their real worth comes from their

Randy Wilson *(center)* and his wife, Lisa, founded the Father Daughter Purity Ball in Colorado in 1998. At the yearly event, fathers pledge to protect the sexual purity of their daughters, who promise to abstain from sex until marriage. Wilson is pictured here with his daughters Jordyn *(left)* and Khrystian *(right)* at the 2007 purity ball. The virginity movement has caught on around the country and is observed primarily by conservative Christians. Some studies have shown that most girls who pledge abstinence do not actually keep their promise and are often less prepared to practice safe sex when they do break the pledge.

status as sexual objects. (Virgins are sexual objects in that they are defined by whether or not they have had sex with a man.) The purity movement defines who they are and how "good" they are. As in porn culture, their sexuality does not belong to them. It belongs to deep-rooted sexist traditions that persist into the twenty-first century.

OBJECTS OR SUBJECTS?

Author Ariel Levy says women share the blame for porn culture, or what she calls "raunch culture." In her 2005 book *Female Chauvinist Pigs,* she singles out celebs she views as some of the most brazen offenders of that time. Her list includes celebrities such as Paris Hilton, Brittney Spears, and Christina Aguilera, to name a few. These days, feminist bloggers also point at figures such as Miley Cyrus, Nicki Minaj, and Katy Perry. These celebrities, say some feminists, contribute to the sexual objectification of women rather than freeing them from it.

WORKING BREASTS

The Victorian era, in the late nineteenth century, is remembered as one of the most sexually repressed times in US history. Forget twerking—just a lady's exposed ankle or wrist could bring on raised eyebrows. And yet, in that buttoned-up age, women freely breast-fed their children in public, even at church.

Compare that to the twenty-first century, in which breast-feeding discrimination has a long history of legal cases. Even though public breast-feeding is legal in all fifty states, nursing mothers are routinely asked to cover up or to go elsewhere. Lactivists are feminist activists who work to raise awareness of the issue. One favorite strategy is for mothers to stage nurse-ins at restaurants, malls, and other establishments that have discouraged public breast-feeding.

Why are nursing breasts such a distasteful sight when breasts are spilling out everywhere in American media culture? Feminists have an answer. A nursing mother's working breast is totally free of sexual connotation. That's offensive to porn culture, which tells women their only value is to be sexy.

Breast-feeding in public, although legal, is a controversial issue in many countries, including the United States. For example, in this 2013 protest in Sydney, Australia, mothers gather outside a café where an employee asked a breast-feeding woman to stop nursing her baby. Feminists feel that porn culture contributes to the over-sexualization of the female breast.

This list of celebrities raises some tricky questions. First, how is pointing at these women any different from slut-shaming—that time-worn practice of shaming women who dare to flout traditional views of female sexuality? Are Levy and those who agree with her reviving old-school sexism by putting down women who celebrate and claim to be defining and taking the best advantage of their own sexuality? Second, aren't these celebrities freely creating their own images—having fun and making a ton of cash while they're at it?

After all, *subjectification* is also a feminist concept. When women are subjects in media, they are in charge. We see things from their point of view. Pop culture experts often point to Madonna as a prime example of a celebrity who is the subject of her own media image. The pop singer's music and videos, in particular, crackle with sexuality that many view as distinct, creative, and ever-changing. It seems to express her individual, authentic desire rather than that of porn culture—and she seems to be the one driving her own image machine.

Levy argues that female chauvinist pigs aren't expressing genuine sexuality. She's not slut-shaming them. She's calling out their sham. These raunch culture divas are perpetuating the one-dimensional, misogynistic image (woman as sex bomb) that stands for sexy in our culture. They're tapping into an illusion of power—individual, fleeting power that's enacted at the expense of other women. The perks vanish with weight gain, pregnancy, disability, and aging.

A GIRLIE POINT OF VIEW

This is where Girlies—those who promote a pro-beauty, pro-femininity type of feminism—might step in and say, "Hold on." If beauty and hotness, as defined by heterosexual standards, are two sources of power for women, why shouldn't they make the most of it? It's not the way it used to be in the bad old days. Beauty and eroticism are just a couple of the many forms of power available to women, say Girlie feminists. Most of all, they say, feminists don't need to get self-righteous about other women's choices.

Storm Large is a lounge singer who has cultivated a retro, sexy vibe, due, in part, to breast enhancement surgery. After her operation, she remembers getting condescending reactions from some women. They accused her of defiling her body and conforming to a heterosexual male standard of sexual beauty. Large says she loves her enhanced curves and gratefully accepts the boost it has given her career.

In the 1995 Third Wave classic book, *To Be Real: Telling the Truth and Changing the Face of Feminism,* Rebecca Walker interviewed supermodel Veronica Webb about what it's like to live and work inside the beauty industry. Webb recounted how she was often personally attacked for setting impossible beauty standards. Women blamed *her* if their boyfriends posted her picture on their bedroom walls. Webb called out a double standard in the way she was treated. Why was it that Arnold Schwarzenegger (a bodybuilder at that time) didn't get criticized in the same way, even though he embodied a physique that most men couldn't live up to either? We all

In an effort to challenge conventional beauty standards and to promote a variety of social concerns, beauty pageant organizers around the world are reshaping the way societies define beauty. For example, the Miss Landmine Angola pageant draws attention to the beauty of women who have been crippled by land mine injuries in decades of civil war there. In 2008 Paulina Vadi *(right)* and Ana Diogo *(left)* were among the ten contestants.

ON DISPLAY

Here are five quick telltale signs to help you think about whether images of a woman in ads on television, in print, or online may be objectifying her. Use the list for analyzing music videos too.

1. The woman's face is turned away from the camera or hidden, often by long hair.
2. Only body parts—usually breasts, hips, and buttocks—are shown.
3. The woman is visible through a window or in a mirror, as if she doesn't know she's being watched.
4. The woman's expression is empty.
5. Her body language is submissive. She's draped over something or flung across a surface with arms and legs splayed. Her lips are usually parted.

have special gifts and talents, she argued. Why should she be expected to hold hers back?

Webb envisioned a future when beauty and sexuality aren't such loaded issues for women. In a truly feminist world, women of all stripes and sizes—including supermodels—will be free to express their varied beauty and sexuality as they see fit, not as they feel pressured by society or economics to do. A postfeminist world will allow women and girls to love their bodies as they are—and their minds—and to feel valued for both.

rEPRODUCTiVE JUSTICE

On a summer day in 2013, Wendy Davis, a state senator from Fort Worth, Texas, catapulted herself into the national spotlight and into feminist stardom. On the morning of June 25, on the floor of the state senate in Austin, Texas, Davis took off her professional shoes and put on a pair of hot pink running sneakers. Her day's work was going to require some serious physical endurance. For the next thirteen hours, she would have to stay on her feet without taking a sip of water or a bathroom break. She could not lean on anything for support. Most challenging, she was to speak nonstop in opposition to a senate bill that proposed the strictest limits on abortion that Texas had seen since 1973. In that year, abortion became a woman's constitutionally protected right in the landmark US Supreme Court case known as *Roe v. Wade*.

Davis's plan was to filibuster Texas Senate Bill 5. A filibuster is a disruptive tactic that legislators use to control legislative proceedings. If Davis could manage to follow the strict rules of filibustering, she would be able to hog the floor of the state senate until midnight when the senate shut down for the session. If she could achieve this, she would prevent a vote on the bill—at least for the time being—and make a powerful statement about her views in support of abortion.

Texas state senator Wendy Davis *(left)* gives the victory sign with her Democratic colleague Senator Jose Rodriguez after the Democrats defeated an antiabortion bill in the state legislature in June 2013. Davis's lengthy filibuster was headline news across the country and contributed to the defeat. Later that summer, however, another version of the bill was passed into law.

Davis knew her only hope was to delay the bill. The eventual passage of the bill into law would be a slam dunk for Texas's ruling Republican majority, who staunchly reject abortion. But by holding off the vote, Davis could draw national attention to an issue that is deeply troubling to women's rights activists and to health-care providers around the United States.

Davis began her filibuster at 11:18 a.m. in front of a packed gallery of supporters. Throughout the day, some 180,000 people from all over the nation watched a live stream of her nonstop speech. Several hours in, she put on a back brace to help stay upright.

Davis lasted almost eleven hours, when the lieutenant governor shut her down for veering off topic. After that, her allies in the state senate took over, while the crowd chanted, cheered, and waved their sneakers in the air. The vote was delayed until two minutes after the midnight deadline. As expected, though, a version of the bill passed handily in Texas later that summer.

INCREASING RESTRICTIONS

Senate Bill 5 was one of many bills put forth across the nation by American activists and politicians opposed to abortion. Since the *Roe* decision, antiabortion lawmakers have not been able to ban abortion outright.

Instead, they have developed a very successful strategy of limiting a woman's access to the procedure and restricting the procedures that physicians can use to perform it. The first major victory was the Hyde Amendment, first passed in 1976, which denies federal funding for abortion. This law impacts poor women in particular because they depend on government money (Medicaid dollars) to pay for their health needs, which may include abortion. With the Hyde Amendment, millions of poor women cannot afford an abortion.

After passage of the Hyde Amendment, states began to pass into law a wide range of additional restrictions. By the twenty-first century, new laws

THE MORNING-AFTER PILL

One long-standing area of disagreement in the arena of reproductive rights has circled around emergency contraception (EC), also known as Plan B One-Step, or the morning-after pill. This controversial medication is for women and teen girls who have had unprotected sex. If taken within seventy-two hours of sex, the medication reduces a woman's chance of getting pregnant by up to 95 percent.

EC can prevent a woman from ovulating or it can disrupt fertilization. It can also prevent a fertilized egg from implanting in the walls of the uterus. For those who believe that life begins at the moment of conception (when egg and sperm meet), EC is a form of abortion. According to medical definitions, however, pregnancy does not begin until implantation.

EC is an over-the-counter medication, available without a prescription to people of any age. In a handful of states, individual pharmacists can call upon what's known as a conscience clause. They can refuse to dispense the pill based on their individual religious beliefs. Feminist advocates of reproductive rights feel this infringes on a woman's freedom to take necessary medication.

Only one in four American teens knows about EC. According to one study, EC could potentially reduce abortion in the United States by two million procedures a year. Advocates are pushing for policies that educate more women about EC, such as requiring emergency rooms to inform rape survivors about the pill and offering it at no cost.

in most states required a twenty-four-hour waiting period before an abortion. When the woman signs up at a clinic for an abortion, a staff member is legally required to hand her a brochure with information about fetal development, adoption, and claims—many of which have no basis in medical research—that link abortion to breast cancer. Some state laws require her to have an ultrasound to see the fetus up close. If the woman is a minor, she will most likely need a written note from her parents giving their consent for their daughter's abortion. All of these laws are meant to dissuade a woman from going through with the abortion.

Feminists oppose these restrictions. They view the laws as condescending to women, who they feel know how to make up their own minds about this personal, private decision. Furthermore, policy experts at the nonprofit Guttmacher Institute point out that the restrictions aren't actually causing women to change their minds. Instead, women are only delaying abortions. When they eventually make their way back to a clinic, they may be much farther along in their pregnancy, when the procedure becomes more invasive, potentially more dangerous to the mother, and much more expensive. Guttmacher research also notes that such laws affect rural women the most. Rural women who do not have access to a clinic in their area must drive several hours to a city clinic. They will typically need to ask for more time off work. They may need to pay for child care while they are gone, as well as for gas, food, and a hotel stay. Feminists believe these are punitive burdens. They point out that most minors do tell their parents if they are seeking an abortion. If they don't, they likely have a good reason not to, such as incest or the threat of physical abuse from a parent or guardian who may become enraged at the news of a teen pregnancy.

TRAP Laws

The Texas bill against which Davis filibustered took a new tactic in restricting access to abortion. As a Targeted Regulation of Abortion Providers (TRAP) bill, it targeted health-care clinics that provide abortions rather than women seeking the procedure. In the United States, almost all abortions take place at freestanding clinics, not at hospitals. In more than 99 percent of all abortions, according to the Guttmacher Institute, first-trimester abortion is a simple medical procedure performed during the first twelve weeks of pregnancy without serious medical complications.

Texas's TRAP bill and others like it require that abortion clinics meet the health and safety standards of ambulatory surgical centers (same-day surgery centers). Texas's forty-one abortion clinics have to be outfitted as hospitals. To do so, they faced millions of dollars in renovation for requirements such as wider hallways, new airflow systems, and locker rooms with showers for doctors, among other requirements. The American College of Obstetricians and Gynecologists (ACOG) and other medical associations object to TRAP laws, saying they have "no medical basis" and serve only to restrict a woman's access to safe and effective abortion.

For some clinics, the expenses brought on by TRAP laws are so high the facilities shut down. By the fall of 2014, only eight abortion clinics in Texas were still standing. Before the law, some 10,000 Texas women had to travel more than 200 miles (322 kilometers) for an abortion. A year later, that number had skyrocketed to 750,000 women.

POVERTY AND ABORTION

As with other abortion restrictions, Texas law hits poor women the hardest. For this reason, health officials fear that some poor women may try to self-abort or turn to illegal, back-alley providers. In both cases, experts point out that the risk of infection and death is significant. The World Health Organization estimates that globally some forty-seven thousand women die each year from unsafe abortions, and millions more are injured.

And Third Wave feminists say that poor women are four times as likely as middle-class women to seek an abortion. In the United States, women—especially women of color—are more likely to be poor than men and make up two-thirds of adults living in poverty. While African American women comprise 13 percent of women overall, they receive 30 percent of abortions.

REPRODUCTIVE JUSTICE

For decades, Second Wave feminists framed the abortion issue in terms of individual choice and privacy. With the *Roe* decision, a woman had the constitutional right to make personal decisions about her reproduction without government restrictions. "Keep your laws off my body!" the protest signs in favor of legalizing abortion said.

Since then Third Wave feminists point out that choice is a complex concept that's influenced by social issues such as class and race. Loretta Ross is a leading member of SisterSong, a feminist group that looks at women's reproductive issues from the point of view of women of color. She explains:

> *Every woman who is pregnant wonders if she has a bedroom for that child; can she afford to take off the time to raise that child? Why flatten the decisions around abortion to just choice? When women don't have jobs or health care, where is the choice? There is nothing worse than a woman aborting a baby she wanted because she couldn't support it.*

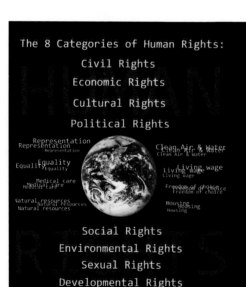

The 8 Categories of Human Rights:

Civil Rights
Economic Rights
Cultural Rights
Political Rights

Representation
Clean Air & Water
Equality
Living wage
Medical care
Freedom of choice
Natural resources
Housing

Social Rights
Environmental Rights
Sexual Rights
Developmental Rights

WWW.SISTERSONG.NET

SisterSong has eighty grassroots organizations in the United States representing five primary ethnic populations/indigenous nations: American Indian/Indigenous, Black/African American, Latina/Puerto Rican, Arab American/Middle Eastern, and Asian/Pacific Islander, as well as white allies and men. The group launched in 1997 to work for reproductive rights and sexual health for women of color. This poster lists eight categories of human rights that SisterSong feels are critical to ensuring those goals.

FEMINISTS FOR LIFE

Can you be a feminist and be pro-life too? For decades most feminists answered this question with a flat-out no. They believed that the legal right to abortion is central to a woman's control of her own life and therefore central to a feminist point of view. And many feminists felt that the pro-life movement did not do enough to fight poverty and to address environmental issues, all of which impact women and children's quality of life.

Some Third Wave feminists, including Jennifer Baumgardner, are evolving their views on the topic of abortion. They point out that Third Wave feminism is all about empowering women to make up their own minds on issues, including abortion. Baumgardner believes feminists have the right to feel queasy about abortion and to express their reservations.

Feminists for Life is one group that has openly opposed abortion since the early 1970s. But unlike traditional pro-life groups, they do not seek to criminalize the procedure. Their mission is to fight the root causes of abortion, such as poorly paying jobs, lack of affordable day care, lack of affordable housing, and other obstacles to ensuring that every pregnancy is a wanted pregnancy. "Abortion is a reflection that we have not met the needs of women," say Feminists for Life posters. "Women deserve better than abortion."

Racism.

Gender bias.

Religious bigotry.

Pregnancy discrimination
is equally wrong—and illegal.

Feminists for Life believes that women should not feel forced to sacrifice their children for an education or a career.

Stand up for women. Join us now.

Refuse to Choose.® • Women Deserve Better.®

FEMINISTS FOR LIFE
OF AMERICA
feministsforlife.org

Feminists for Life opposes abortion and works toward values that support and accept pregnancy and motherhood. This poster focuses on pregnancy discrimination, which although illegal, still happens when pregnant women are not hired, are fired, or are in some way discriminated against because they are pregnant or have recently had a baby.

Ross is a pioneer of the reproductive justice movement, a cause founded by women of color in the 1990s. As its name implies, reproductive justice combines traditional issues of reproductive rights, such as abortion and contraception, with issues of social justice, such as affordable housing, day care, and health care.

Reproductive justice activists advocate for a woman's control of her "reproductive destiny." Women have the "right to have children, not have children, and to parent the children [they] have in safe and healthy environments," regardless of race, disability, and sexual orientation.

Activists for the movement believe that the role of the US government is to respect a woman's privacy to make her own decisions about abortion as well as to play an active role in helping women with other reproductive issues. For example, the government would ensure that women who want to have babies can afford to do so through raising the minimum wage and enacting other labor and tax policies that distribute wealth more evenly across society. The government can also play a role in funding and promoting good schools, day care centers, and neighborhood clinics. It's a lot like the government's role in the airplane industry, Ross says. The US government can't force you to fly or not to fly. It doesn't tell you where to go. But it has an obligation to make sure flights are safe, affordable, and accessible for those people who choose to fly.

FORCED STERILIZATION

The reproductive justice movement grew out of a rift between mainstream, white feminists and feminist women of color. In the 1960s and 1970s, women of color were facing forced sterilization—a medical procedure that prevents a woman from ever having children. In one of the most regretted chapters in feminist history, white feminists didn't step up to speak out against the procedure.

The history of forced sterilization goes back to the early twentieth century, when a panic spread through white, Protestant America. As increasing numbers of new immigrants came to the United States from Asia and southern Europe, many white Americans feared being racially outnumbered. In response, various states introduced eugenics (selective breeding) laws to sterilize those people deemed "unfit" for breeding. The unfit included immigrants, people of color, and the disabled, among others.

After World War II (1939–1945), with the horrors of Adolf Hitler's eugenics campaign against Jews and other minority groups in Europe, eugenics laws were removed from the books in the United States. However, informal sterilization practices took over. Under the guise of fighting poverty, government-paid doctors at public clinics and hospitals routinely coerced African American, Latina, and American Indian women to be sterilized "for their own good." For examples, some doctors pressured women to consent to the procedure during the throes of childbirth. Doctors lied or pressured women through exaggerated threats. They told poor women they would lose their welfare benefits unless they agreed to the procedure and threatened American Indian women with having their children taken away. Spanish-speaking women signed English-language forms consenting to sterilization that they didn't fully understand. In one famous case from 1973, a pair of teen sisters in Alabama were sterilized without their parents' knowledge or consent.

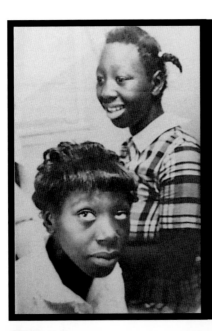

In 1973 the Southern Poverty Law Center sued what is now the Department of Health and Human Services on behalf of Mary Alice and Minnie Relf *(left)*. The teens were involuntarily sterilized in Alabama when they were fourteen and twelve, respectively. As a result of the lawsuit, doctors were required to obtain informed consent before any sterilization procedure.

Meanwhile, a white middle-class woman who wanted to be sterilized had to get an official OK from two doctors and a psychiatrist. In addition, she had to meet the 120 formula: her age times the number of children she already had could not equal less than 120. That meant that a thirty-year-old white woman needed to have four children to be considered for the procedure.

In 1978, under pressure from activist groups such as the Committee to End Sterilization Abuse, the US government instituted waiting periods and other guidelines to protect against forced sterilization. Yet mainstream white feminists cried foul. They argued that government regulations such as these interfered with a woman's personal choice about sterilization. They did not take into account that forced sterilization had left more than 25 percent of American Indian women infertile, effectively wiping out some smaller tribes. In the US territory of Puerto Rico, one-third of the women of childbearing age there had been sterilized.

THE RIGHT TO BE MOTHERS

Reproductive justice activists fiercely protect a woman's right to be a mother. In the 1990s, they fought a battle against long-acting contraception, such as Norplant and Depo-Provera, drugs that a doctor can inject or implant under the skin. Like the pill, these methods use hormones to prevent pregnancy, but they last for years and are far less safe than the pill. Even so, health workers pushed them on poor women of color. For example, government-funded clinics offered Norplant to low-income women for free but did not offer other, shorter-acting birth control methods.

By 2002 Norplant's maker Wyeth-Ayerst was tangled in so many lawsuits by women who had been harmed by the unsafe contraceptive that the drug manufacturer took Norplant off the US market. The painful history of forced or coercive sterilization is largely a thing of the past, but feminists still watch for cases of abuse. In 2013 the Center for Investigative Reporting broke open a story about illegal sterilization at California prisons. Between 2006 and 2010, medical staff at two California prisons pressured 148 female inmates to undergo the procedure. Prison doctors skirted or found ways to avoid the required approval process to perform such an operation. For example, in at least one case, the doctor got around the paperwork by documenting the operation as a medical emergency.

In the twenty-first century, feminists protect motherhood in varied ways. The agenda ranges from ending adoption discrimination against same-sex couples to fighting racism in the child protection system, which overwhelmingly removes black children from their families in response to allegations of abuse. (About 37 percent of children in foster care are black, though black children make up only 15 percent of US children.) It encompasses a movement by American Indian women to return to traditional birthing methods and to ensure the rights of incarcerated mothers to deliver their babies in prison hospitals without being chained to the delivery table. The movement also pushes for caring treatment programs that help pregnant women who are addicted to drugs get sober rather than criminalizing them for their addiction disease.

Activists within the reproductive justice movement are also concerned about the increasing rate of fatal pregnancies among US women. The rate more than doubled between 1990 and 2013, with African American women dying from pregnancy and childbirth nearly four times as often as their white counterparts. Researchers identify a web of causes, most notably limited access to affordable, high-quality health care.

INFERTILITY

Third Wave feminists also work on the issue of infertility. In the United States, infertility rates are higher among women of color than white women. According to the National Survey of Family Growth, black married women are twice as likely to face infertility as white women. What's the cause?

A sexually transmitted infection is one cause. Chlamydia, in particular, hits African Americans hard. A black person is eight times more likely to be infected by the infection than a white person. Left untreated, chlamydia can lead to infertility in women and it may damage men's fertility as well. But why is it left untreated among women of color? It's because of poor access to health care. Why do women of color get more STIs in the first place? Again, poor access to health care. And lack of comprehensive sex education is another known contributor to high STI rates. Many people don't know how to protect against these diseases. STIs spread faster among communities with a higher rate of untreated individuals. Researchers have even linked the problem to the epidemic number of black men in prison. The women left behind find new sexual partners who may have untreated STIs, and the untreated infections spread rapidly.

Environmental toxins also cause infertility, and women of color are exposed to disproportionately high levels of pollution. They are more likely to hold low-paying jobs at nail salons, factories, dry cleaners, and other workplaces that expose workers to hazardous chemicals. Their neighborhoods are more likely to sit dangerously close to landfills, power plants, or industrial waste sites that pollute the air and water. For example, in two-thirds of Latino communities in the United States, air quality does not meet US government safety standards.

The example of infertility, with its myriad causes, shows why reproductive justice activists often refer to the feminist theory of intersectionality. It points to why reproductive rights activists in the twenty-first century engage on so many fronts. Wages, education, health care, pollution, criminal justice, cultural norms—all these and more limit or expand a woman's control of her reproductive destiny.

CHAPTER SiX

WHAT'S NEXT?

The driving principle of Wellesley College, founded in Massachusetts in 1870, has been to empower women. At this exclusive women's college, students are often called sisters, and *she* has been the universal pronoun in official documents. In the past few years, however, students such as Timothy Boatwright are calling out the college's assumptions. Boatwright is transgender. He was raised a girl and applied to the college as a female. For a long time, he secretly considered himself "masculine-of-center genderqueer."

Boatwright sought out the women's college because of his transgender identity. He felt he'd be more accepted in a feminist space. After all, feminism and the transgender movement share a philosophical outlook: both reject the notion that a person's biology determines what you can be.

Boatwright transitioned formally to a masculine identity after he'd already been accepted to Wellesley as a woman, and the college allowed him to stay after the transition. Life as a *he* at Wellesley went OK until the spring of 2014, when Boatwright decided to run for student government. An anonymous Facebook campaign sprang up, urging Wellesley students to block Boatwright's run. Wellesley wasn't founded to launch men into positions of power, his opponents argued.

Wellesley College is a women's college in Massachusetts. Timothy Boatwright, born female, transitioned to a masculine identity in 2013 while a student there and was allowed to stay. In 1968 the college held its annual hoop-racing contest *(left)*. The winner of the race in 2014 was Alex Poon, the first transgender student to win the race. His mother had won the same race in 1982.

Boatwright was running for the student government job of multicultural affairs coordinator, to represent minority interests on campus. Of all people, he knew what it was like to be a minority at the school, he argued. In the end, Wellesley's students overwhelmingly supported him and Boatwright won by a landslide.

GENDER JUSTICE

As ideas about gender shift, colleges and universities across the United States are scrambling to figure out how to keep up. Their positions are all over the map, with some schools digging in their heels with strict gender-specific policies and others embracing all gender variant people and their needs. This issue reflects a wider conversation within the feminist movement. Should feminism focus squarely on women or widen the net as broadly as possible? Most feminists don't want to repeat past mistakes by excluding any minority group. They see trans people as natural allies in the fight for gender justice.

Feminists have long asserted that rigid gender roles harm all people. For many, the next step is to dismantle the gender binary—the system that sets up masculine and feminine as the only two options for defining gender identity.

TRANSGENDER AMERICA

Gender identity is a person's inborn sense of being a man or a woman, masculine or feminine—or neither. For cisgender people, the sex of their bodies (male or female) and their brains match up with their gender identity. Transgender people feel that the sex of the body they were born with does not fit how they perceive their gender. Transgender people identify outside of the gender binary, the system that allows for only two opposite gender identities, masculine and feminine.

Some transgender people undergo gender confirmation procedures to match their bodies with their gender identity. They do this in consultation with a medical team that provides hormone therapy and surgeries. Other people choose only to change their name or the way they dress or to switch the pronouns they use to talk about themselves. Instead of "he" or "she," they may prefer the gender-neutral "zhe" or "hir." Some trans people go back and forth between genders. They sometimes refer to their gender identity as genderqueer. Just as feminists fight sexism, the trans movement fights gender entitlement. That's the idea that some gender expressions are more "normal" or "natural" than others.

In May 2014, *Time* magazine featured a trans person on its cover for the first time in its history. Actress Laverne Cox provided a face to a movement the magazine called the nation's next civil rights frontier. From former Olympian athlete Caitlyn Jenner to *Dancing with the Stars* celebrity Chaz Bono, trans Americans are gaining visibility in the culture

Olympic athlete Caitlyn Jenner, formerly known as Bruce Jenner, accepts the Arthur Ashe Courage Award at the 2015 ESPYS in Los Angeles. The award goes to people, often top athletes such as Jenner, whose contributions have gone beyond the sporting world.

and telling their stories in their own words. They are seeing everyday changes as high school students vote to elect trans prom kings and queens, universities and retail spaces add gender-neutral bathrooms, and towns and cities revise their policies to make it easier for trans people to change their genders on birth certificates and other official documents.

Actor Emma Watson summed up this viewpoint in a 2014 speech to kick off the United Nations' HeForShe campaign, a program that calls upon men and boys to promote gender equality:

> If men don't have to be aggressive in order to be accepted, women won't feel compelled to be submissive. If men don't have to control, women won't have to be controlled. Both men and women should feel free to be sensitive. Both men and women should feel free to be strong. . . . It is time that we all perceive gender on a spectrum, not as two opposing sets of ideals.

ONLINE REVOLUTION

Some feminists question whether gender is the most appropriate focus for twenty-first-century feminism. Does working to update notions of gender foster reproductive justice? Will it raise the minimum wage or end police brutality against women of color? What about double standards, beauty standards, fat-shaming, harassment, maternity leave, day care, dress codes, doulas, STIs, the wage gap, stalkers, streetwalkers, and sex ed? What are feminism's priorities?

As the movement shifts to the Internet, it's getting harder to take its pulse. Blogs and websites from *Jezebel* to *Double X* to *Feministing, Autostraddle, Black Girl Dangerous, The Bad Dominicana, Hollaback!* and hundreds more offer a breathtaking array of feminist issues. These sites also act as watchdogs, calling out sexism in the culture. *Hollaback!* provides a space for women to share their personal stories of sexual harassment, for example, while *Jezebel* has posted "before" images of photoshopped celebrities.

FOURTH WAVE FEMINISM: GOING VIRAL

The Internet also offers powerful organizing tools. After police arrested Debra Harrell for neglecting her daughter in a city park, a supporter on YouCaring.com crowdsourced more than $45,000 for the struggling single mother. Livestreams of Wendy Davis's filibuster mesmerized viewers across the nation. The Texas state senator shot into the national spotlight, allowing her to make a bid for governor in 2014.

Online protests have also sparked real change. Disney pulled a line of *Avengers* T-shirts that said "I Need a Hero" for girls and "Be a Hero" for boys after feminist activists challenged the sexism of the message through tweets and petitions. Why can't girls be heroes too? #FreetheNipple got Facebook to stop censoring photos posted by breast-feeding mothers. In 2012 MoveOn.org collected more than eight hundred thousand signatures after the Susan G. Komen foundation—the largest and best-funded breast cancer research foundation in the United States—decided to stop giving money to Planned Parenthood. The breast cancer research group had pulled funding because of pressure from antiabortion groups that didn't feel the money should go to an organization that educates men and women about abortion. Online feminism turned out to be the more forceful influence. Within just three days, the Komen foundation reversed its decision. Komen leaders admitted that they had made a huge public relations blunder, and the group's founder, Nancy Brinker, stepped down as CEO. Even so, donations to the foundation dipped by $77 million the next year.

With the Internet, feminist discourse has never been more widespread, democratic, and robust. Some people are even calling Internet feminism the Fourth Wave. Internet feminism makes the Third Wave goal of inclusivity even more practical and accessible. A quick Google search allows feminists with every outlook to join in communities or organize with like-minded thinkers. If the Third Wave introduced do-it-yourself feminism, the Fourth Wave took DIY to another level, where anyone with an Internet connection and a bit of savvy can start a protest, begin a conversation, or make an artistic statement about a deeply held belief.

But not all feminists are so smitten with the new feminist cybersphere. Some online feminist critics and scholars point out that the exciting online universe is also muddled and chaotic. Like-minded thinkers can find one another, but they can also fracture off into isolated groups. In this context, Internet feminism becomes an echo chamber of repeating ideas. Without the benefit of rich and challenging discussion, these ideas don't evolve or deepen. Feminist activists Courtney Martin and Jessica Valenti, for example, point to their own experiences with hateful, angry, online commentary, some from other feminists or from people who feel excluded. Additionally, some critics feel that online feminism enables "slackervists," who want to indulge in feel-good feminism without any real personal stake and without taking any real action.

Within this whirlwind, feminism can get pretty confusing. Just look at the example of Beyoncé. Google the pop star's 2014 MTV Video Music Awards performance to see her dance in front of the word *feminist* in lights. Google her again to see her pole dancing. What's the message? Does it matter? Feminism has never benefited from turning away from contradiction. Maybe the Fourth Wave's most important task is simply to prop open the door. Young people leap or step into feminism's halls, as noisy and wandering as they might be.

Facing questions about her feminist credentials, megastar Beyoncé *(above)* wrote an essay about gender inequality in 2014 for the *Shriver Report*. The nonpartisan organization had conducted research showing that forty-two million women in the United States either live in poverty or are close to it. Beyoncé wrote about her views of how men and women can work to achieve gender equality and the challenges that face them in reaching that goal.

A Feminist Wish List

Feminism has racked up some stunning victories since the mid-nineteenth century. What are some feminist hopes for the next century? Twenty-first-century feminists have a wide range of goals. Put together, they look like this:

- People of all genders and races vigorously debate policy in the highest levels of government and business. Leadership is not a boys-only club.
- Americans elect female presidents.
- Beauty standards are accepting of the wide range of human bodies.
- Movie heroes and celebrity heartthrobs of all stripes hold us spellbound with their dazzling diversity of identities. Hollywood is not a boys-only club.
- Women are creators of art as often as they are its subjects. Women no longer routinely hide behind long tresses of hair or play peek-a-boo with the camera.
- Universal health care pays for abortion and birth control.
- Minimum wage laws provide a full-time worker with enough money to pay the bills, feed a family, and save a little bit of money for the future.
- Domestic workers (who are no longer mostly women) make as much money as garbage collectors (who are no longer mostly men).
- Women get equal pay for equal work. They earn one hundred cents for every dollar earned by men.
- Women say "I'm sorry" only when they should be. So do men.
- Women are valued for their intelligence and sense of humor more than for their sex appeal.
- Stay-at-home fathers don't get a second glance at playgrounds. Caring for kids is not a girls-only club.

- Guaranteed paid family leave, paid sick time, and day care funded by the government are all givens for anyone in the workplace, just like social security.
- Homemakers receive social security benefits for their years of work.
- Sexual violence and domestic abuse are rare crimes, met with swift justice.
- Women fill STEM jobs. Being an engineer or a computer software developer is no longer a boys-only club.
- A women's basketball team with a winning record sells more tickets than a losing men's team.
- Schools don't need a special Women's History month anymore to focus on women's achievements. Women's contributions are covered thoroughly in history class throughout the year.
- Add your own: _____.

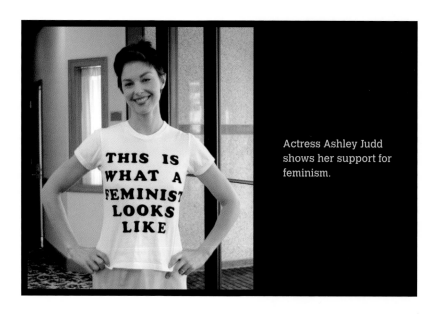

Actress Ashley Judd shows her support for feminism.

TIMELINE

1848 In the Declaration of Sentiments and Resolutions, compiled at the woman's rights convention in Seneca Falls, New York, feminism's founding mothers kick off the First Wave by riffing on the Declaration of Independence: "We hold these truths to be self-evident: that all men *and women* are created equal."

1851 Sojourner Truth speaks up for black women with her groundbreaking "Ain't I a Woman?" speech in Akron, Ohio.

1916 In New York City, Margaret Sanger opens the first birth control clinic in the United States and is jailed for doing so.

1920 The Nineteenth Amendment to the US Constitution is ratified, granting American women the right to vote.

1960 The FDA approves the Pill.

1963 Betty Friedan's *The Feminist Mystique* captures—and revolutionizes—the way white, middle-class housewives view the limits on their lives. Under the Equal Pay Act, bosses can no longer pay a woman less than a man for doing the exact same job.

1964 The first shelter for domestic abuse victims opens, in California. Title VII of the Civil Rights Act of 1964 prohibits job discrimination on the basis of sex.

1968 Shirley Chisholm becomes the first African American woman to serve in the US Congress. Protesters at the Miss America Pageant in Atlantic City, New Jersey, propel feminism into the national spotlight.

1971 *Our Bodies, Ourselves,* a groundbreaking manual of women's health and sexuality, is published.

1972 Gloria Steinem and Dorothy Pitman Hughes cofound *Ms.* magazine. Under Title IX, schools can't discriminate on the basis of sex, opening the door for organized girls' sports.

1973 In *Roe v. Wade,* the US Supreme Court rules that first-trimester abortions are constitutionally protected—legal—in all states.

1978 Congress outlaws job discrimination against pregnant women.

1981 Sandra Day O'Connor becomes the first female Supreme Court justice.

1983   Sally Ride becomes the first American female astronaut.

1985   The Guerrilla Girls begin their masked mission to publicly humiliate racist and sexist leaders of the arts community.

1992   Rebecca Walker coins the term *Third Wave,* writing in *Ms.* magazine, "I am not a postfeminism feminist. I am the Third Wave." The Third Wave Direct Action Corporation, launched by Rebecca Walker and Shannon Liss, kicks off its mission of funding broad social justice projects led by young women.

2004   Massachusetts becomes the first state to legalize same-sex marriage.

2011   After a Toronto, Ontario, police officer remarks that women shouldn't dress like sluts if they don't want to be raped, some three thousand Canadian activists launch the first SlutWalk.

2013   The US military changes regulations to allow women to serve in direct combat roles.

2014   California passes the nation's first "Yes means yes" law for college campuses, expanding the definition of rape to meet feminist standards. Under "Yes means yes," a sexual encounter is not considered consensual (voluntary) unless both parties verbally agree to have sex with each other.

2015   The comedy world sees a new generation of edgy, groundbreaking female comics, including Amy Schumer, Adrienne Truscott, Ilana Glazer, and Abbi Jacobson. The US Supreme Court rules in favor of same-sex marriage.

FEMINIST TERMS

beauty cult: a feminist term for the way popular culture sets up impossible standards of beauty. The beauty cult drives high rates of eating disorders and plastic surgery among women and girls.

Bechdel Test: three criteria for evaluating the extent to which a movie incorporates female characters. To pass, a movie must include 1) two female characters with names, 2) who speak to each other, and 3) in a conversation that is not about the male characters.

emergency contraception: also known as the morning-after pill. Emergency contraception is medication that can prevent a pregnancy if taken within seventy-two hours after unprotected sex.

gender binary: a social construct that sets up masculine and feminine as the only two options for defining gender identity

gender entitlement: the notion that one's own gender identity is more "natural" or "better" than someone else's

genderqueer: people who don't think of themselves as either masculine or feminine. Their gender identity lies somewhere in between or may change from time to time.

intersectionality: a word to describe how multiple forms of oppression, such as racism and sexism, overlap in women's lives

maternal wall: the combination of social forces, including expensive day care and inflexible work cultures, that keep mothers from advancing to high-paying, powerful positions in the workforce

misogyny: hatred or contempt for women

mommy tax: a term coined by writer Ann Crittenden to describe how women's incomes fall once they become mothers

objectification: treating a human being like an object, which has no feelings, intelligence, or point of view

patriarchy: a society controlled by men and masculinity

pay gap: the difference in pay between an average full-time female worker and an average full-time male worker in the United States. In 2015 women earned, on average, seventy-eight cents for every dollar earned by men.

"Personal is political": the Second Wave feminist revelation that what happens to women in their private lives, such as pregnancy and domestic violence, are part of larger social problems with political solutions

porn culture: a strain of pop culture that glorifies stereotypical heterosexual male standards of "sexiness" for women and values women only by those standards. Feminists argue that porn culture sets up unrealistic standards of what constitutes "hot" for women and that it interferes with the development of girls' healthy sexuality.

pornography: movies, pictures, magazines, and films featuring naked people, sex, or both to cause sexual excitement

rape culture: the feminist idea that sexist and misogynistic social attitudes cause and perpetuate rape

Targeted Regulation of Abortion Providers (TRAP) laws: laws that require abortion clinics to meet the standards of hospitals. Under these laws, many abortion clinics have had to shut down because they cannot afford to meet the regulations.

Title IX: the 1972 federal law that prohibits sex discrimination in schools that receive government funding. Title IX paved the way for girls' participation in school sports.

transgender: a person whose gender identity does not match with the sex assigned at birth or with the anatomical sex and reproductive features of that person's body

"Yes means yes!": a feminist revision of the "No means no!" standard of defining rape. Also known as affirmative consent, "Yes means yes!" says that sexual consent requires more than just the absence of the word *no* to reject a sexual encounter. It requires a clear yes from partners to express willingness to have sex.

FEMINIST THINKERS AND PIONEERS

Betty Friedan (1921–2006)

In 1963 Betty Friedan published *The Feminine Mystique,* a book that shattered the myth of the happy housewife and is credited with kick-starting feminism's Second Wave. As Friedan's book flew off shelves, she rose in prominence as a women's rights activist. In 1966 she helped found the National Organization for Women, which is still the largest feminist organization in the United States. A strong supporter of abortion rights, Friedan also helped found in 1969 the National Association for the Repeal of Abortion Laws, today known as NARAL Pro-Choice America. Friedan was from Peoria, Illinois.

bell hooks (1952–)

Born Gloria Jean Watkins in Hopkinsville, Kentucky, bell hooks doesn't capitalize her pen name because she wants to underscore the importance of the texts she writes, not herself as an author and a thinker. She has written a breathtaking array of texts, from poetry and children's books to feminist manifestos. Her 1981 book *Ain't I a Woman? Black Women and Feminism* broke open a conversation about how racism and sexism overlap in black women's lives. In 2011 *Ms.* readers voted hooks's 2000 book *Feminism Is for Everybody* as the top nonfiction feminist book of all time.

Adrienne Rich (1929–2012)

Born in Baltimore, Maryland, Adrienne Rich began her adult life as a conventional 1950s wife and mother who also wrote beautiful formal poetry. But Rich's life and art would completely transform with her self-awakening in the 1960s. Rich is remembered as a lesbian feminist thinker and preeminent American poet who intimately connected her art to her own radical viewpoints. In 1997 Rich famously refused the US government's prestigious National Medal of Arts award in protest of a government she felt put power in too few hands. "[Art] means nothing if it simply decorates the dinner table of the power which holds it hostage," Rich said.

Margaret Sanger (1879–1966)

Sanger, from Corning, New York, was the founder of the reproductive rights movement in the United States. Sanger's own mother underwent eighteen pregnancies before she died at the age of forty. This spurred Sanger's unwavering passion to make birth control available to women at a time when doing so was against the law. Sanger invented the term *birth control* in 1916. In 1921 she founded the American Birth Control League, which went on to become Planned Parenthood. In the last decade of her life, Sanger pushed for the invention of the birth control pill—a dream she saw realized in 1960.

Julia Serano (1967–)

On her website juliaserano.com, Julia Serano describes herself as "a true Renaissance woman." Though she is known widely in the San Francisco area as a poet, musician, and spoken word artist, Serano is recognized nationally as a pioneering trans feminist. Her 2007 book *Whipping Girl: A Transsexual Woman on Sexism and the Scapegoating of Femininity* is becoming required reading in dozens of gender studies courses across the nation. *Ms.* magazine readers voted it No. 16 in a list of 100 nonfiction feminist classics. Serano is from Philadelphia, Pennsylvania.

Elizabeth Cady Stanton (1815–1902)

Born in Johnstown, New York, Stanton is best remembered as the author of the Declaration of Sentiments and Resolutions, the 1848 document that declared women's rights to vote and own property and kicked off the First Wave of US feminism. Stanton wrote widely on many feminist issues, including a woman's right to ride a bicycle. As a mother of seven, Stanton wasn't as free to travel as her friend and fellow First Wave suffragette Susan B. Anthony, who had no children. Anthony delivered many of the speeches Stanton wrote—and got much of the accompanying fame.

Gloria Steinem (1934–)

A Second Wave icon, Gloria Steinem helped found *Ms.* magazine in 1972. The glossy, mass-circulation magazine was the first of its kind, and it brought feminism into the homes of millions of American women. An articulate speaker with a glamorous image, Steinem served as the face of feminism in pop culture for several decades. In 2009 Steinem said, "We've demonstrated that women can do what men do, but not yet that men can do what women do." She continues her work to break down rigid gender roles for both men and women. Steinem is from Toledo, Ohio.

Rebecca Walker (1969–)

Rebecca Walker was just twenty-two when she coined the term *Third Wave* and invigorated a generation of feminists who both passionately believed in the movement and saw a need for change. "To be a feminist is to integrate an ideology of equality and empowerment into the very fiber of my life," Walker wrote. "It is to . . . join in sisterhood with women who are divided [and] to understand power structures with the intention of challenging them." A few years later, Walker put her words into action by cofounding what would become the Third Wave Fund. The group promoted women's rights with the larger context of social justice issues. Walker went on to write several books including her 2001 memoir *Black White and Jewish.* Her more recent work, including the 2007 book *Baby Love: Choosing Motherhood after a Lifetime of Ambivalence,* addresses issues of motherhood, family, and romantic love. Walker is from Jackson, Mississippi, and is the daughter of feminist writer Alice Walker and lawyer Melvyn Leventhal.

SOURCE NOTES

9–10 "The New Do: Calling Yourself a Feminist," *Glamour*, accessed July 10, 2015, http://www.glamour.com/inspired/2013/09/the-new-do-calling-yourself-a-feminist.

10 Katie McDonough, "I'm Not a Feminist, but . . .," *Salon*, April 6, 2013, http://www.salon.com/2013/04/06/im_not_a_feminist_but/http://www.salon.com/2013/04/06/im_not_a_feminist_but/.

10 "Feminism," *Merriam-Webster.com,* accessed July 10, 2015, http://www.merriam-webster.com/dictionary/feminismhttp://www.merriam-webster.com/dictionary/feminism.

12 Jennifer Baumgardner, *F'em! Goo Goo, Gaga, and Some Thoughts on Balls* (Berkeley, CA: Seal, 2011), 11.

12 Ibid., 147.

12 Rory Dicker, *A History of U.S. Feminisms* (Berkeley, CA: Seal, 2008), 18.

13 bell hooks, *Feminism Is for Everybody: Passionate Politics,* 2nd ed. (New York: Routledge, 2014), 1.

13 Dicker, *A History of U.S. Feminisms*, 20.

13 "Caitlin Moran > Quotes," *Goodreads.com,* accessed July 10, 2015, http://www.goodreads.com/author/quotes/939363.Caitlin_Moran.

15 Jennifer Baumgardner and Amy Richards, *Manifesta: Young Women, Feminism, and the Future* (New York: Macmillan, 2000), 83.

20 "The Declaration of Sentiments and Resolutions Seneca Falls Conference (1848)," McCarter Theatre Center, accessed July 10, 2015, http://www.mccarter.org/education/mrs-packard/html/MRS.%20PACKARD%20The%20Declaration%20of%20Sentiments,%20Seneca%20Falls%20Hyperlink.pdf.

20–21 Julie Zeilinger, *A Little F'D Up: Why Feminism Is Not a Dirty Word* (Berkeley, CA: Seal, 2012), 27.

24 "The American Experience: Miss America," *PBS*, accessed July 10, 2015, http://www.pbs.org/wgbh/amex/missamerica/peopleevents/e_feminists.html.

28 Lisa Jervis and Andi Zeisler, eds., *Bitchfest: Ten Years of Cultural Criticism from the Pages of Bitch Magazine* (New York: Farrar, Straus and Giroux, 2006), 106.

28 Rebecca Walker, *To Be Real: Telling the Truth and Changing the Face of Feminism* (New York: Anchor, 1995), xxiii.

30 Baumgardner and Richards, *Manifesta*, 56–57.

33 Jennifer Van Laar, "South Carolina Mom Learns the Hard Way If You Drop Your Kid Off at a Playground, You Can Go to Jail," *Independent Journal Review,* accessed July 13, 2014, http://www.ijreview.com/2014/07/156818-let -child-play-park- unsupervised-go-jail/.

39 Anne-Marie Slaughter, "Why Women Still Can't Have It All," *Atlantic,* July/ August 2012, http://www.theatlantic.com/magazine/archive/2012/07/why -women-still-cant-have-it-all/309020/.

41 Joan Blades and Kristen Rowe-Finkbeiner, *The Motherhood Manifesto: What America's Moms Want and What to Do about It* (New York: Nation, 2006), 4.

42 "Administrator Lisa P. Jackson, Remarks at the New Jersey Women of Distinction Awards, as Prepared," EPA, March 11, 2012, http://yosemite.epa .gov/opa/admpress.nsf/a883dc3da7094f97852572a00065d7d8/e6ecb4867a7df63 2852579bf006f6d21!OpenDocument.

44 "California Gunman Suspect's 'Retribution' Video," *Washington Post,* May 24, 2014, http://www.washingtonpost.com/politics/elliot-rodgers-killing-spree -what-happened/2014/05/24/207778ec-e3b2-11e3-810f-764fe508b82d_story.html.

44 Jessica Valenti, "Elliot Rodger's California Shooting Spree: Further Proof That Misogyny Kills," *Guardian* (Manchester), May 24, 2014, http://www.theguardian .com/commentisfree/2014/may/24/elliot-rodgers-california-shooting-mental -health-misogyny.

45 Conor Friedersdorf, "Normal Violence in a Murder Spree," *Atlantic,* May 25, 2014, http://www.theatlantic.com/national/archive/2014/05/women-react-to-a -murder-spree-at-ucsb-with-an-airing-of-grievances/371568/.

45 Alan White, "Twitter Responds to Santa Barbara Shootings with #YesAllWomen Hashtag," *BuzzFeed,* May 25, 2014, http://www.buzzfeed.com /alanwhite/twitter-responds-to-santa-barbara-shootings-with-yesallwomen.

45 Friedersdorf, "Normal Violence."

45 Ibid.

45 Ibid.

45 Nolan Feeney, "The Most Powerful #YesAllWomen Tweets," *Time,* May 25, 2014, http://time.com/114043/yesallwomen-hashtag-santa-barbara-shooting/.

45 Ibid.

47 "The Cards," *Cards against Harassment,* accessed July 10, 2015, http://www .cardsagainstharassment.com/cards.html.

51 Jaclyn Friedman and Jessica Valenti, eds., *Yes Means Yes! Visions of Female Sexual Power & a World without Rape* (Berkeley, CA: Seal, 2008), 217–218.

56   "Rape and Sexual Assaults," *Our Bodies, Ourselves*, October 15, 2011, http://www.ourbodiesourselves.org/health-info/rape-and-sexual-assault/

57   Baumgardner, *F'em! Goo Goo,* 234.

57   Karen F. Balkin, ed., *Violence against Women: Current Controversies* (Farmington Hill, MI: Greenhaven, 2004), 35.

58   Margaret Hartmann, "Kelly Clarkson Slimmed Down on Self via Photoshop," *Jezebel,* August 7, 2009, http://jezebel.com/5332409/kelly-clarkson-slimmed-down-on-self-via-photoshop.

59   "Photoshopping: Altering Images and Our Minds," *Beauty Redefined* (blog), March 12, 2014, http://www.beautyredefined.net/photoshopping-altering-images-and-our-minds/.

62   Renee Engeln, "An Epidemic of Beauty Sickness," TEDx video, 15:47, October 21, 2013, http://tedxtalks.ted.com/video/An-Epidemic-of-Beauty-Sickness.

62   Ibid.

63   "Caitlin Moran > Quotes," *Goodreads.com.*

63   Jervis and Zeisler, *Bitchfest,* 257.

63   "The Dangerous Ways Ads See Women—Jean Kilbourne—TEDxLafayetteCollege," YouTube video, 15:51, posted by "TEDx Talks," May 8, 2014, https://www.youtube.com/watch?v=Uy8yLaoWybk.

64   Barbara Findlen, ed. *Listen Up! Voices from the Next Feminist Generation* (Emeryville, CA: Seal, 2001), 106.

65   Ibid., 108.

65   "Cutie Mark Magic," Hasbro, accessed July 11, 2015, http://www.hasbro.com/mylittlepony/en_US/play/details.cfm?R=26F66F35-5056-9047-F536-384C3BC7AD7F:en_US.

66   "These Are the Victoria's Secret Items for Teens That Parents Are Furious About," *Business Insider,* accessed July 11, 2015, http://www.businessinsider.com/victorias-secret-teen-line-pink-2013-3#another-one-says-take-me-to-paradise-2.

66   Zayda Rivera, "Nicki Minaj Talks, 'Anaconda,' Music Video Controversy: 'It's Just Cheeky, Like a Funny Story,'" *New York Daily News,* October 20, 2014, http://www.nydailynews.com/entertainment/gossip/nicki-minaj-talks-anaconda-video-cheeky-article-1.1980608.

69   "Ariel Levy on 'Raunch Culture,'" *Independent* (London), December 4, 2005, http://www.independent.co.uk/news/uk/this-britain/ariel-levy-on-raunch-culture-517878.html.

78   "ACOG and AMA File Amicus Brief in Planned Parenthood v Abbott," ACOG, December 20, 2013, http://www.acog.org/About-ACOG/News-Room/News-Releases/2013/ACOG-and-AMA-File-Amicus-Brief.

79   Jennifer Baumgardner, *Abortion and Life* (New York: Akashic, 2008), 67.

80   "Our Mission," *Feminists for Life,* accessed July 11, 2015, http://www.feministsforlife.org/our-mission-organization/.

81   "What Is RJ?," *SisterSong,* accessed July 11, 2015, http://sistersong.net/index.php?option=com_content&view=article&id=141&Itemid=8.

86   Ruth Padawer, "When Women Become Men at Wellesley," *New York Times Magazine,* October 15, 2014, http://www.nytimes.com/2014/10/19/magazine/when-women-become-men-at-wellesley-college.html.

89   Amanda Marcotte, "Emma Watson Threatened with Nude Photo Leak for Speaking Out about Women's Equality," *Slate,* September 22, 2014, http://www.slate.com/blogs/xx_factor/2014/09/22/emma_watson_attacked_after_un_speech_on_feminism_4chan_users_threaten_to.html.

90   Elizabeth Plank, "23 Inspiring Feminist Digital Campaigns That Changed the World," *Mic,* February 7, 2014, http://mic.com/articles/80229/23-inspiring-feminist-digital-campaigns-that-changed-the-world.

94   Declaration of Sentiments and Resolutions, The Elizabeth Cady Stanton & Susan B. Anthony Papers Project, accessed July 11, 2015, http://ecssba.rutgers.edu/docs/seneca.html.

95   Estelle B. Freedman, ed., *The Essential Feminist Reader* (New York: Modern Library, 2007), 401.

98   "Adrienne Rich," *poets.org,* accessed July 11, 2015, http://www.poets.org/poetsorg/poet/adrienne-rich.

99   "About Julia," *JuliaSerano.com,* accessed July 11, 2015, http://www.juliaserano.com/about.html.

99   "Gloria Steinem Biography," *Biography.com,* accessed July 11, 2015, http://www.biography.com/people/gloria-steinem-9493491.

99   Barbara Ryan, *Identity Politics in the Women's Movement* (New York: NYU Press, 2001), 80.

SELECTED BIBLIOGRAPHY

"Backlash Book Club." *Matter,* August 12, 2014. https://medium.com/@readmatter
/backlashbookclub-c303e57f5230.

Balkin, Karen F., ed. *Violence against Women: Current Controversies.* Farmington Hill,
MI: Greenhaven, 2004.

Baumgardner, Jennifer. *Abortion and Life.* New York: Akashic, 2008.

———. *F'em! Goo Goo, Gaga, and Some Thoughts on Balls.* Berkeley, CA: Seal, 2011.

Blades, Joan, and Kristen Rowe-Finkbeiner. *The Motherhood Manifesto: What
America's Moms Want and What to Do about It.* New York: Nation, 2006.

Boston Women's Health Book Collective. *Our Bodies, Ourselves.* New York:
Touchstone, 2011.

Cheney-Rice, Zak. "American Healthcare Is So Bad for Women of Color It May Violate
the UN Convention." *Mic*, September 18, 2014. http://mic.com/articles/99148
/american-healthcare-is-nbsp-so-awful-for-women-of-color-it-may-violate-the
-un-convention.

Coates, Jennifer. *Women, Men and Language: A Sociolinguistic Account of Gender
Differences in Language.* Harlow, UK: Pearson Education, 2004.

Cohen, Nancy L. *Delirium: The Politics of Sex in America.* Berkeley, CA: Counterpoint,
2012.

Dicker, Rory. *A History of U.S. Feminisms.* Berkeley, CA: Seal, 2008.

Findlen, Barbara, ed. *Listen Up! Voices from the Next Feminist Generation.* Emeryville,
CA: Seal, 2001.

Freedman, Estelle B., ed. *The Essential Feminist Reader.* New York: Modern Library,
2007.

Friedman, Jaclyn, and Jessica Valenti, eds. *Yes Means Yes! Visions of Female Sexual
Power & a World without Rape.* Berkeley, CA: Seal, 2008.

Fudge, Rachel. "Everything You Always Wanted to Know about Feminism but Were
Afraid to Ask." *Bitch Magazine.* Accessed March 14, 2015. http://bitchmagazine
.org/article/everything-about-feminism-you-wanted-to-know-but-were-afraid
-to-ask.

hooks, bell. *Ain't I a Woman: Black Women and Feminism.* Boston: South End, 1981.

Jervis, Lisa, and Andi Zeisler, eds. *Bitchfest: Ten Years of Cultural Criticism from the
Pages of Bitch Magazine.* New York: Farrar, Straus and Giroux, 2006.

Labaton, Vivien, and Dawn Lundy Martin, eds. *The Fire This Time: Young Activists and
the New Feminism.* New York: Anchor, 2004.

"Maze of Injustice: The Failure to Protect Indigenous Women from Sexual Violence in the USA." Amnestyusa.org. Accessed June 5, 2015. http://www.amnestyusa.org/pdfs/mazeofinjustice.pdf.

Rosin, Hanna. *The End of Men and the Rise of Women.* New York: Riverhead, 2012.

Serano, Julia. *Whipping Girl: A Transsexual Woman on Sexism and the Scapegoating of Femininity.* Berkeley, CA: Seal, 2007.

Silliman, Jael, Marlene Gerber Fried, Loretta Ross, and Elena Gutierrez. *Undivided Rights: Women of Color Organize for Reproductive Justice.* Cambridge, MA: South End, 2004.

Slaughter, Anne-Marie. "Why Women Still Can't Have It All." *Atlantic,* July/August 2012. http://www.theatlantic.com/magazine/archive/2012/07/why-women-still-cant-have-it-all/309020/.

Solinger, Rickie. *Reproductive Politics: What Everyone Needs to Know.* New York: Oxford University Press, 2013.

Solnit, Rebecca. *Men Explain Things to Me.* Chicago: Haymarket, 2014.

Traister, Rebecca, and Judith Shulevitz. "Feminist Has Conquered the Culture. Now Comes the Hard Part." *New Republic,* September 14, 2014. http://www.newrepublic.com/article/119412/feminisms-future-debate.

Valenti, Jessica. *Full-Frontal Feminism: A Young Woman's Guide to Why Feminism Matters.* Berkeley, CA: Seal, 2007.

Walker, Rebecca. *To Be Real: Telling the Truth and Changing the Face of Feminism.* New York: Anchor, 1995.

FURTHER INFORMATION

Books

Baker, Jean H. *Margaret Sanger: A Life of Passion*. New York: Hill and Wang, 2011.

Baumgardner, Jennifer, and Amy Richards. *Manifesta: Young Women, Feminism, and the Future*. Reprint. New York: Farrar, Straus and Giroux, 2010.

Behnke, Alison Marie. *Up for Sale: Human Trafficking and Modern Slavery*. Minneapolis: Twenty-First Century Books, 2015.

Bornstein, Kate, and S. Bear Bergman. *Gender Outlaws: The Next Generation*. Berkeley, CA: Seal, 2010.

Carter, Jimmy. A *Call to Action: Women, Religion, Violence, and Power*. New York: Simon & Schuster, 2014.

Colman, Penny. *Elizabeth Cady Stanton and Susan B. Anthony: A Friendship That Changed the World*. New York: Henry Holt, 2011.

Cronn-Mills, Kirstin. *Transgender Lives: Complex Stories, Complex Voices*. Minneapolis: Twenty-First Century Books, 2015.

Gay, Roxanne. *Bad Feminist*. New York: Harper Perennial, 2014.

Harding, Kate, and Amanda Hess. *The Book of Jezebel: An Illustrated Encyclopedia of Lady Things*. New York: Grand Central, 2013.

hooks, bell. *Feminism Is for Everybody: Passionate Politics*. Cambridge, MA: South End, 2000.

Kristof, Nicholas, and Sheryl WuDunn. *Half the Sky: Turning Oppression into Opportunity for Women Worldwide*. New York: Knopf, 2009.

Morgan, Joan. *When Chickenheads Come Home to Roost . . . My Life as a Hip-Hop Feminist*. New York: Simon & Schuster, 1999.

Wittenstein, Vicki Oransky. *Reproductive Rights: Who Decides?* Minneapolis: Twenty-First Century Books, 2016.

Zeilinger, Julie. *A Little F'd Up: Why Feminism Is Not a Dirty Word*. Berkeley, CA: Seal, 2012.

Websites

AAUW—Economic Justice Page
http://www.aauw.org/research/the-simple-truth-about-the-gender-pay-gap/
AAUW breaks down the latest numbers behind the gender pay gap and brings them to life with clear analysis and personal stories.

The F Bomb
http://thefbomb.org/
Third Waver Julie Zeilinger started this online community for teen feminists. The F Bomb invites readers to submit poetry, articles, and short essays.

Feminist.com—Articles & Speeches

http://www.feminist.com/resources/artspeech/

Read selections from classic feminist texts on a range of subjects, including several chapters from the latest updated version of *Our Bodies, Ourselves*.

Mic

http://mic.com/identities

Read news and think pieces aimed at millennial feminists, with beautiful graphics and photos.

Rookie

http://www.rookiemag.com/

A lifestyle magazine for teenage girls, *Rookie* covers everything from fiction, tech, art, and more, all with a feminist sensibility.

Videos and Documentaries

"Emma Watson HeForShe Speech at the United Nations." YouTube, 11:47. Posted by "HeForShe," September 22, 2014. https://www.youtube.com/watch?v=Q0Dg226G2Z8. See the speech that went viral in 2014.

Feminist Frequency Video Blog

http://feministfrequency.com/

Check out Anita Sarkeesian's filmed critiques of female images in video games that rocked the online gaming world. Sarkeesian's work has earned her a spot on *Time* magazine's 100 Most Influential People of 2015.

The Hunting Ground. Directed by Kirby Dick. New York: RADiUS-TWC, 2015. (PG-13) Oscar-nominated filmmaker Kirby Dick presents an exposé of sexual assault on US campuses. This investigative documentary follows the lives of several survivors as they struggle to pursue justice in the aftermath of their attacks.

Miss Representation. Directed by Jennifer Siebel Newsom. New York: Virgil Films & Entertainment, 2011. (NR) This documentary film examines the US media's limited and skewed portrayals of girls and women.

The Punk Singer. Directed by Sini Anderson. New York: Sundance Selects, 2013. (NR) Riot Grrrl pioneer, lead singer of Bikini Kill, and Third Wave icon Kathleen Hanna stars in this documentary about her own life.

"We Should All Be Feminists" YouTube video, 34:41. Posted by "Sarge WP," May 4, 2014. https://www.youtube.com/watch?v=hg3umXU_qWc. See the talk by famed Nigerian novelist Chimamanda Ngozi Adichie that Beyoncé sampled on "***Flawless."

TAKE ACTION

Advocates for Youth

2000 M St. NW, Suite 750
Washington, DC 20036
http://www.advocatesforyouth.org
Advocates for Youth helps young people make informed decisions about their reproductive health based on the 3Rs—rights, respect, and responsibility. Go to the "Youth Activism" section for dozens of ways to get involved, including becoming a trained youth activist. Link to their sister sites for specific campaigns, including MySistahs.org (for young women of color), YouthResource.org (for GLBTQ youth), and AmbienteJoven.org (for Spanish-speaking GLBTQ youth).

Feminists for Life (FFL)

PO Box 320667
Alexandria, VA 22320
http://www.feministsforlife.org
Feminists for Life is an organization that works to reduce abortion by giving expectant mothers the resources they need to continue their pregnancies. In their "Tools for Schools" section, FFL offer free resources to set up an information table. They also share ideas for what individuals can do to help, such as offering free babysitting for a mother in need.

Geena Davis Institute on Gender in Media

4712 Admiralty Way
Suite 455
Marina Del Rey, CA 90292
http://seejane.org
The institute, founded in 2004 by actor Geena Davis, is a research-based organization within the media and entertainment industry that works to educate and influence industry leaders and followers to improve gender balance, reduce stereotyping, and create diverse female characters in entertainment aimed at children eleven years old and younger. The site offers opportunities to volunteer as well as information for parents, teachers, and kids.

INCITE!

2416 W. Victory Blvd.
Burbank, CA 91506
http://www.incite-national.org/home
Find an INCITE! local chapter or partner group and connect with other young activists to fight violence against women and trans people of color.

NARAL Pro-Choice America

1156 15th St. NW, Suite 700
Washington, DC 20005
http://www.prochoiceamerica.org
NARAL is a grassroots feminist organization that focuses on abortion rights and women's reproductive health. Click on the "Get Involved" button to find opportunities ranging from joining social media campaigns to volunteering in your area.

National Center for Transgender Equality

1325 Massachusetts Ave. NW, Suite 700
Washington, DC 20005
http://transequality.org
This national advocacy group for trans people and their allies has a special request for trans youth. Go to their website and share your story or fill out the US Trans Survey. One of the organization's most vital projects is documenting and giving a voice to trans Americans.

National Organization for Women (NOW)

1100 H St. NW, Suite 300
Washington, DC 20005
http://now.org
NOW is the largest organization of feminist activists in the United States, with some five hundred chapters on campuses and cities in all fifty states. Join a chapter or find out how to add your voice to one of their dozens of national awareness campaigns.

Third Wave Fund

PO Box 1159
Brooklyn, NY 11238
http://Thirdwavefund.org
The Third Wave Fund is a resource for youth who are already active in a social justice cause. The group connects young feminist, queer, and trans organizers with donors interested in funding their projects.

PHOTO ACKNOWLEDGMENTS

The images in this book are used with the permission of: © iStockphoto.com/ksushsh (paper background); © iStockphoto.com/Tolga_TEZCAN (torn paper piece); © iStockphoto.com/pkanchana, p. 1; © RetroRF/Getty Images, p. 5; AP Photo, pp. 6, 25; Kyndell Harkness/Minneapolis Star Tribune/MCT/Collection/Newscom, p. 7; © Alistair Berg/Getty Images, p. 9; © David M. Benett/Getty Images for Universal Pictures/Glamour Magazine, p. 13; REUTERS/Jose Luis Quintana, p. 17; © Kean Collection/Getty Images, p. 19; Library of Congress (LC-USZ62-20176), p. 21; © National Portrait Gallery, Smithsonian Institution/Art Resource, NY, p. 26; © Bettman/CORBIS, p. 27; © Brian Velenchenko/CORBIS, p. 29; © M.Sobreira/Alamy, p. 30; © RF Corbis Value/Alamy, p. 33; © Harry E. Walker/MCT/Getty Images, p. 35; © Peter Cade/Iconica/Getty Images, p. 37; Pete Souza/White House/Sipa Press/Newscom, p. 38; © Kevin Foy/Alamy, p. 53; © Andrew Burton/Getty Images, p. 55; © Dimitrios Kambouris/WireImage/Getty Images, p. 59; akg-images/Newscom, p. 61 (left); © Logopedia/Wikimedia Commons, p. 61 (right); © Independent Picture Service, p. 65; © Denise Truscello/Getty Images for Madame Tussauds Las Vegas, p. 66; © Michael Graham-Stewart/Bridgeman Images, p. 67; Rick Wilking/Reuters/Landov, p. 69; © Tamara Dean/The Sydney Morning Herald/Fairfax Media/Getty Images, p. 70; CB2/ZOB/WENN/Newscom, p. 72; © Erich Schlegel/Getty Images, p. 75; via SisterSong, p. 79; via Feminists for Life of America, p. 80; via Museum of Disability, p. 82; © William Ryerson/The Boston Globe/Getty Images, p. 87; © Kevin Winter/Getty Images, p. 88; © Jason LaVeris/FilmMagic/Getty Images, p. 91; © Paul Natkin/Getty Images, p. 93.

Front cover: © iStockphoto.com/omergenc (fist); © iStockphoto.com/Tolga_TEZCAN (paper piece); © iStockphoto.com/pkanchana (sun burst retro background).

Jacket flaps: © iStockphoto.com/ksushsh (paper background); © iStockphoto.com/Tolga_TEZCAN (torn paper piece).

Back cover: © iStockphoto.com/pkanchana (sun burst retro background); © iStockphoto.com/ksushsh (paper background); © iStockphoto.com/Tolga_TEZCAN (torn paper piece).

ABOUT THE AUTHOR

Nadia Abushanab Higgins is the author of some ninety books for children and young adults. A die-hard researcher, she has written about everything from ants to planets to zombies. Her fiction series, Fiona & Frieda's Fairy-Tale Adventures, retells classic fairy tales with a feminist twist. Higgins lives in Minneapolis, Minnesota, with her husband and two daughters.

INDEX